The Grace is Ours

The Loving Light Books Series

Also by Liane Rich

Loving Light

Book 20

The Grace is Ours

Liane Rich

Loving Light Books
Original Copyright © 1998
Copyright © 2012 Liane

ISBN 13: 978-1-878480-20-0
ISBN 10: 1-878480-20-0

Loving Light Books:
www.lovinglightbooks.com

Also Available at:
Amazon: www.amazon.com
Barnes & Noble: www.barnesandnoble.com

Grace is the presence of light. You are in a state of grace when you are in light, which is love....

for Nancy

The information in this series is not necessarily meant to be taken literally. It is meant to *shift* your consciousness...

Foreword

Anyone immersed in the vast body of new metaphysical knowledge is aware of the virtual symphony of voices from channeled sources throughout the world – inspirational voices that may be artistic, poetic, philosophical, religious, or scientific. And now, out of these myriad New Age voices, comes a series of books by God, channeled through Liane, revealing the frank truth in all its glory and wonder, telling us how to cleanse our bodies, gain access to our subconscious minds, clear our other selves and march back to who we are – God.

In God's books you will be introduced to a loving, powerful, gripping, exciting, and often humorous voice that reaches out and speaks ever so personally to the individual reader. As the reader's interest deepens, invariably an intimate relationship to this voice develops. It is a relationship that lasts forever, and I am quite certain I do mean forever.

Here is an accelerated program, a no-holds-barred course, where God guides us and loves us, and as needs be recommends books to us and even a movie or musical piece along the way. He (She) enters our lives and sees through our eyes, seeming to enjoy the ride as He guides us back to US, back to ALL. Here is a voice that is playful and informative, that is humorous and serious, that is gentle and powerfully divine. It is a voice that knows no barriers or restrictions, a straightforward and honest voice that caresses us when we need the warmth and pushes us when we are immobilized.

In today's New Age literature there is an avalanche of information from magnificent beings of light, information that possesses us and compels us to look at our fears and express our love. In this series of books by God, you will find truly powerful methods for making this transition from toxicity to purity, from density to light, from fear to love, and from the delusion of death to the awakening to full life. You will experience in these books the love and the power of God for it is your love to express and your power to behold. Rarely will you see more lucid steps for transformation. Read these beautiful words and rejoice in our period of awakening, our return to Home.

John Farrell, PhD., LCSW. – Psychologist, Clinical Social Worker, Senior Clinician Psychiatric Emergency Services, U.C. Davis Medical Center, Sacramento. John is also a retired Professor – California State University, Sacramento, in Health Sciences and Psychology.

The Grace is Ours

Introduction

As long as you have peace you will have love! So; how does one create peace? We get out of the way and *allow* it to enter our lives. We do not block peace out of a need to be free of peace; however, we do block peace out of fear. We fear everything we do not understand. Mostly you fear your own feelings. You fear loneliness and you fear congestion in your lives. You want to be alone and left alone and yet you fear being alone. You are not so much out of touch with fear as you think. You are fear because you think of fear. When you no longer think of fear, you will let it go back into balance.

Most of you do not require peace you only require less fear. When less fear has been added, you will be less fearful and less confused and less unsafe. You will feel whole and accepted by releasing fear. Do you want to release fear? No, you do not. You are afraid that if you let go of fear, it will take over. At least, with you holding it, it gives you the "illusion" that you are in control. So; does fear have you or do you have it? Is it in control of you or are you in control of it? Is it you, or are you it? Who is it? Does it live without you, or does it exist because of you? How does it work? How does it grow? How can it sustain itself without the help of your thoughts?

You will find that fear is mostly a projected belief regarding what you think, or what another thinks. Fear is mostly a panic point in thought form. It is a slight bit different from pain, in that it travels outside as well as inside of you. Fear is more real and yet just as unreal as pain. Fear can cause pain, as well as stress and illness. Fear is very big, and fear creates more fear by growing and circling and spiraling into space and time. Time covers a lot of space and space covers a lot of time. Together they work to "allow" energy to travel. Space and time are important to the "production" of fear. The greater time and space, the greater room for expansion and development of energy. Time and space require energy to pass through them in order to be of use. Time and space are nothing without energy, just as a bottle is nothing without the liquid it holds. It is useful because of the space inside which gives it a purpose. Its purpose is to hold liquid or whatever is put into it.

Without purpose life dissolves. Everything reacts and interacts with everything else. Every particle is in a position to create just by its presence in the universe. Every spec has a purpose and every spec was created for a reason. When two or more purposes cross they create conflict and often explode into something else, or implode on themselves. This is still purpose and will be viewed as a creative force. Explosions are creative and death is creative. You, however, are so stuck in "fear" of death that you cannot see how everything – absolutely every last little thing has a purpose. When purpose is no longer here, the "thing," whatever form it has taken, will begin to change to something else. *This is creation!*

You do not trust creation and yet you are creation. You are so big and so vast that you are lost in you. This is about to change. Welcome to our last and final book on the subject of God. We will write other books but, for now, you will find this our final book of information in this particular series titled the "Loving Light Books" series. As you read this information know that you have been drawn to this point in your belief and your thoughts for a purpose. This purpose is to "evolve" out of ignorance and fear. It's so easy for you to fear information because you have had all the light pushed out of you in order to make room for fear.

As fear leaves you, you will get you back. You have been possessed for so long that you are afraid to have you back. You are even afraid to be you. Do not despair. We will do all that we can to assist you, and you will know that you have been shown the many faces and aspects of God. God is one. God is all. So far you can only accept a small identity for God. This too shall change.

As we guide you and lead you, I do hope you realize that this is so advanced from what you normally read. This is how to get God back. This is how to get you back. This is how to get love back.

Once you begin to understand energy and how it works, you will begin to understand how you work. You are a "light." You think you are human and solid and hard and dark but, in reality, you are "light." Light is what makes you up and you consist of light energy. You are not so much out of light, or energy, as you are turned-off. You must turn-on in order to see. You cannot see when you are turned-off. Once you adapt to being turned-on, you will begin to allow parts that are turning you off to fall away. Mostly you are being blocked by these parts. Anyone who has asked to be brought to the light will begin to travel "in" to the light. This means going through the turned-off parts to get to the turned-on part of you. This part is in the center of you, and as you travel through the parts that have been shut down and turned-off, you will "experience" them.

This means that those who ask to see the light get to see the dark first. If you have been asking and you are not to your center yet, do not fear. Light is in you, and your "desire" to receive light will eventually bring it to you or, better put, bring you to it. It takes time, and I will remind you that instant gratification is a byproduct of ignorance. If you need it so desperately "right now" it would be yours "right now." You do not need the light "right now." What you need "right now" is movement. When you feel fear move in you, celebrate! When you feel pain move in you, celebrate! When you feel the awfulness move in you, celebrate! These things have been so blocked, and frozen in you, for life after life after life. You are finally moving this energy for the first time in a very, very long time. This is the process of returning to the light. Once you allow darkness to move, it can leave you. If you never want it to move, you will be stuck in it just as it is stuck in you.

You are all coming to a point of congratulations. You are all learning to move energy that you find unbearable and undesirable. You are learning to turn you on by allowing energy to move in you and by no longer fearing this energy. You are learning to move to your own center and not be stuck on the outer perimeters of your own beingness. You will begin to use "all" of you instead of just fragments of you. You also learn to allow yourself the time that is required to heal. Instant bliss or gratification is a product of transcendental meditation. It allows you a glimpse of what can be. You can access glimpses to show you how your center feels, and then you must unlock the doors, and allow everything to escape that you have so cautiously and carefully kept a prisoner in you.

Once you unlock your prison doors you may lose your glimpse of instant bliss, but you will regain bliss by allowing all of your demons to speak and by allowing all of your prisoners to be heard from. You are a product of everything that is "in" you, and you are terrified of most of what is "in" you.

Do not judge you, and do not be upset with you if you have been allowing yourself to experience the energy that has for many, many lives been trapped in you. You are turning a corner in the evolution of human beingness, and you are doing it out of "desire," not out of fear of punishment. You are actually, for the first time ever, taking a hand in your own creation. Think of it! God working with man (woman/child). God allowing you to be born unto him. You allowing God to be born unto you!

⚜

Now you are beginning to transform. Now, as you *feel* all that is in you, you will begin the process of change. Change is going to take place because change is all that exists when you are dealing with energy. Even when you block energy it is still moving. It sometimes multiplies itself, and divides itself, and continues to move in directions that you are not aware of. Your only priority seems to be, "Do not let me feel it, or see it, or have to deal with it." Often this creates a pattern that is repeated for many, many lifetimes. I will tell you now that you all hide your emotions, and you all hide what you fear the most.

Do not be upset if you do not transform overnight. You will transform to the degree, and intensity, to which you apply what you have learned so far in your evolution. If your *desire* to not touch "you" (what you are made of) is strong, you will continue to hide most of you. If your *desire* to touch you (and all that you are made of) is strong, you will begin to touch you... all of you... your pain, your fear, your confusion, your dark stored energy.

So; are you upset about touching you? Does it bother you to be feeling you? Or are you beginning to see how releasing these bound-up parts of you will allow you to grow out of pain and confusion and darkness? Do you know how lucky you are if your desire is to see the truth and to know you? Do you realize that this simple process, of owning what is "in" you, will change what is "in" you? You will no longer feel afraid of knowing who and what you are. You will no longer hide from yourself and doubt yourself. You will feel whole and no longer struggle with the process of fragmentation. You will feel powerful being you and no longer feel victimized by you. You will begin to know love (acceptance of the self) and you will begin to know God.

God is total and complete acceptance of everything. Once you begin to accept you and accept your foibles, as well as your strength of character, you will feel so very good. This process is in place to make you like you; to allow you to love you. This process is in place to allow you to feel good about you by showing you where you feel bad about you. This is coming out of karma. This is showing you how to be free of the down-spin cycle and *change* direction to an up-spin cycle. *You will like loving (accepting) you and you will like love.*

∂∬∽

*A*s you learn to let go of what is trapped in you, you will allow yourself to receive. The same barrier that keeps something blocked "in" you is also the barrier that keeps you from receiving. You build a wall to block the wind and it will also block a beautiful sunset or sunrise. You block out what you don't want and you lose what you do want. The only way to free you is to let the walls fall, and this will make you vulnerable. You *hate* to be vulnerable. You all want to be "on top" and "in charge" of your own life, as well as your feelings and emotions.

Once you begin to knock down your walls of protection, you will know it. How? – you ask. You will feel vulnerable. You will feel like you are not "on top" and not "in charge." You will feel lost and confused. The interesting part of knocking down your walls is that you will try desperately to re-establish them the minute they fall. You need your walls. You love your walls. You hide behind your walls. You are lost to God behind your walls.

As you learn to be less aggressive in your defensive behavior, you will automatically loosen your grip on your walls. You will let go of your desperate need to hold your wall in place. For many of you, your wall is the barrier of anger. You use your anger to get yourself motivated and you use your anger to intimidate others, and you use your anger to control both yourself and others. When you let go of this need to be angry, you will receive what is at the other end of anger. Anger is being "displeased." No pleasure! No joy! You are in control.

You hold pleasure and joy at bay in your pursuit for control. In your daily pursuit to control your life and keep it how you want it, you build and establish laws that become rules that become walls of protection. This is not wrong or bad, it is simply how you build walls to protect you. Your walls eventually turn into prisons that block the light and starve you in the process. You are killing you off a little at a time by walling you off in order to protect you. You thought you were doing 'good' and it created an opposite. Whenever you create a "good" way or "right" way, you automatically receive both polarities. Good is only one end of a line that is bad at its opposite. Right is also just one end of a line that has another end. That end is wrong and it opposes right. Now you have a struggle within you over right and wrong, also good and bad.

How can you end this struggle and have peace? Begin to let go of your rules which require rigid walls and strict protection. Deny yourself freedom and you shall be a prisoner. Set yourself free and you shall feel vulnerable for a while, until you can adjust to not having the wall of protection. So; if you feel upset, hurt, vulnerable, and are afraid, you are probably in the process of releasing your hold on a wall of protection. Your walls make you feel safe, but it is a false safety and a false sense of security. You are now moving into a time that will allow you the assistance you require in letting go of false realities. You are beginning to break into "you." You are behind the wall. You have been hidden and "stuck" there for a very long time.

❧❧

*A*s you learn how to "accept" and "embrace" your own parts you will begin to heal! You will begin to see how it is to know all of you instead of fearing all of you. You will begin to manifest from wholeness instead of from fragmentation. I will give you an example: you want to live in a newer home and you have been putting your "thought" energy into creating this new home. You have focused on saving the money you require, and you have even sold a few personal treasures to raise the money you need. You even found the perfect place. Wow! You have "manifested" your dream home. This "creating your own reality" stuff really works for you and you are thrilled! Now, you begin the process of moving. For some reason things hit a snag and the move gets a little complicated, but everything eventually works out. You get moved in and you begin to see a few flaws that you didn't, at first inspection of your new home, notice. Now, however, they seem like glaring projections of unappropriate size.

You are finding faults with your new home, but you bragged to everyone about how you "manifested" just what you wanted for yourself, so you don't want to admit that you now see big flaws in your manifestation. You are embarrassed to admit that all is not well with it. So now you decide to accept your home "as is," and you find it difficult since you are now in the process of a big repair job on this newer, better place to live. What went so wrong with your creation? I will tell you what went wrong. You have unresolved issues with parts of you. These parts are "alive" and create just as you do. They are in you. They are you. They make up a big part of you. They are upset, angry and tired of being pushed away. You don't want to "feel" anything that might cause you to know your own pain. They are your pain, and they have built-up charge to the extent that they may be more powerful at creating than you.

The first thing to do is to get you to stop being upset with this part of you. So I say to you, "let go and let God, go with the flow and do not judge." This allows you to stop condemning these parts further. If you continue to judge them and what they create, you will make them stronger and bigger. The trick is to get them in their right place, which is as a part of you, not as something you reject. They are "in" you, and to reject them pushes them deeper into your psyche where they continue to grow.

So; here is the dilemma: how do I get you to accept all of you? I start by defusing your biggest fears about being you. I start by telling you that you are part of something greater; you are more than you know or think that you are. Then I teach you how to see and accept things that once frightened you. Then I tell you how much I love you for being part of God and allowing God to show you your own fears. Now you are calm enough, and feeling safe enough with this dialogue, that I can begin to point out what is "in" you without you freaking out and hiding deeper in you.

You will learn that all parts of you actually serve a purpose, and you will eventually integrate those you decide to accept and release those you no longer wish to keep. Some are false parts made up of false beliefs from many, many past lifetimes of moral judgments and prejudices. You will not easily access the deeper beliefs until you have released some of the more recent layers which hold them in place. All parts will eventually show themselves and you will eventually know you and integrate most of you, so your manifestations will be created from wholeness, instead of from part of you who really wants to give yourself a gift and part of you who only wants to punish you (for being so hateful as to try for eons to kill off that particular part).

You are now learning about you and how you work. Do not be afraid to know you and to feel unpleasantness. There is much anger in you and anger creates unpleasantness as it goes. It will go as you release your hold on it and you need not judge you,

God, or life for any unpleasantness you experience. You are simply moving energy up and out of you. You are ascending and it takes a little time, at least for the first team. After the first team gets through, things will lighten up for the others who will also know God.

༄

*A*s you begin to recreate your world by recreating your own *perception* of it, you will become a little confused and maybe even upset. You see; you have known what you have known for a very long time. To have someone come along and change what you have known, will only allow you to get more upset and feel less in control. So, do not be upset with yourself when you begin to get upset about changing.

It is very apparent that many of you hate to be wrong; for you believe that when you are wrong you are guilty and must in some form be punished. It is easy to follow the old set of rules and patterns, and it is difficult to get you (your inner workings) to switch over to a new way of doing things. You are so set in your rules (right and wrong) that you do not want to let go of them. In any situation you will find that you love to make someone "at fault." If it is not "you" it will be "them."

It is not possible for you to see how you create greater karma in this way. Karma – meaning "the pattern that continues" or "the cycle that prevails."

Once you learn how to "let go" of right or wrong you will automatically drop blame. Blame does not exist without right or wrong. Blame cannot be without these two energies to support it and feed it. You think that if you accept blame (self-blame) you save yourself from being bad (by judging another). A lot of you actually believe that you are using self-blame to make you a good and honest person. "Well, I'll take the energy here so no one else has to" is not a very good way to view energy. You do not need to take what is not yours. It is not necessary to be "big," or "adult," and accept blame that is not yours. On the other hand, it is not necessary to push or shift the blame for something from one place to the next. Blame doesn't even really exist because there is no "fault," because "everything is perfect," but *you* do not see that.

So; until *you* can see the perfection that exists in everything, I will continue to discuss life with you in terms of right and wrong, good and bad, save you or condemn you. These are terms you *know*. And we all know how "you know what you know."

So; as we learn to redirect your energy and to let go of what you know, you will begin to feel helpless and vulnerable and weak and sad, and after you get sad you will probably get mad and try to "hold-on" instead of "let-go." Do not judge yourself for not wanting to "let go." Nothing is right and nothing is wrong. You are not wrong to get sad or mad. You are not right to get peace and harmony. It only feels better to you because you feel like you are escaping your anger and your more confusing feelings. Once you come to "center," you will experience each feeling for what it is and it will no longer feel good or bad. It will just "be." And to "be" is to flow, and to "flow" is to be part of creation and creator all at once. You cannot perceive the importance of "flowing" at this time, and you do not really understand how to "flow," but it will come slowly and gradually in little ways until it is "all that is."

Once you begin to understand how you are put together, you will begin to understand how you attract what you already are to you. You are not a bag of bones. *You are* information. You are the equivalent of your *experience*. So; what have you experienced and how often and how much? Which lives do you remember? None! How can you not remember who you were before? I will tell you how. You are equipped with a system that "shut down" in order to "tune out" information. What I would like to do is "open" you up so you might begin to know who you are. Once you "open," you will be in a position to allow energy to run both ways... in and out! Right now your blocks are so strong that very little gets in or out of you, and this is, of course, what makes you a big ball of gaseous energy that is slowly destroying who and what you are.

As you learn to develop your ability to "open," you will see how you can defuse you and allow old programming "out." This will allow you to "receive" new energy which is "light." As you receive greater and greater amounts of light, you will be allowed to "see." You do not see! You are blind! If you could see, you would no longer punish you and you would automatically "respect" who you are without any need to achieve a goal, or a title, or fame, or prosperity. You would "see" how you are God, and you would be so full of "light" because you would have let go of *"your need"* for darkness.

You need darkness because you want to hide who you are from yourself as well as from others. The funny thing is that the part you try to hide is what will always come forward because you are pushing it and forcing it to move. You think you can push it down in you, but it will surface because you go "up" you do not go down. You think of yourself as having depth or a bottom to yourself, but you do not go down. You *are* down and you can only go up from where you are. You might say you are on the bottom floor, and you continue to push the elevator button to descend because you do not realize that you have descended as far as you can go. Now it is time to turn around and start focusing on "up." Anything that you push will round out and return. You are at the bottom of your circle or cycle, and you can only round up towards the top again.

Now; for those of you who carry great shame and guilt and continue to draw pain for a punishment of this guilt, you will begin to let go of it all, and you will see it is never necessary to bear guilt, or shame, or anything that has been created out of *your* judgment.

Once you begin to "see," you will automatically be guilt free, which allows you to end punishment. You see, without guilt no one ever deserves punishment. At this point in your evolution you still hang on to good and bad, but that is changing quickly and it frightens you. You will hold on to your blindness concerning guilt until you have had your fill of guilt. Then you will allow something else to run your life. Guilt is the major cause of all pain and suffering. You create from what you carry, and what you are more full of than even fear is the guilt of being bad or going the wrong way. Let it go! There is no bad... there is no wrong way.

So; why do you sit there and suffer year after year? You are full of suffering as it is a direct result of guilt, then pain and punishment. Love it or leave it! You are hooked into it by your fear of accepting everything as good... yes; even death (your biggest fear) is good!

⁂

Once you begin to understand how "idea" is what creates for you, you will begin to know how you created pain. You had this "idea" that a signal for hurting or harming yourself would be a good thing. You began by using small signals, which gradually grew to larger ones in order to send you a much stronger message. Once you were "receiving" a message, you would notice a drop in the level of pain. As you grew more accustomed to pain it did not frighten you so much, and you began to ignore the small signals altogether. Your attention could only be drawn by the larger, longer signals and so this is what we have today. Many of you could have a small signal and not rectify your situation, however, when you have a big, loud, long signal you stop doing whatever it is that is causing your signal.

Say you have to lift a heavy box and you get just a slight twinge of pain for a short instant, this will cause you no concern. However, if you lift the heavy box and you receive a pain signal that lasts for several hours, you will be more likely to stop and allow that back of yours the time it requires to heal whatever needs healing. It fixes itself you know! The body can and once did repair itself in most instances. All of that has changed with the creation of medicine and surgery, and all those wonderful pills you take without knowing what they might do to you in the long run. Anyway, at one time it all ran fairly smoothly and the pain signal was a good "idea." Now it no longer works so well and most of you are so full of pain, both emotional and physical, that it is very difficult for you to clear it all.

There are many ways to create your reality, and one way is to release your hold on pain. You hold on to pain in the same way that you hold on to fear. It has become so big in you that it feels, at times, that life is painful. Life is not meant to be painful. It is simply that your pain energy is big "in" you, and like attracts like. The way to release pain is to ask it to surface. This is difficult, simply because pain will feel like pain when it surfaces. You do not require a "new life" or a "new body" so much as you require the release of pain.

☙❧

As you become more and more accustomed to being human as well as God, you will find it easier to accept all parts of you. You are God and you are man. The God of you does not judge and does not worry, the man or woman of you does. To be human, or to *become* human, you must take on human traits. If you were to become a cat or a dog, you would not take on human traits and inhabit a human form. You would take on the trait of the species you chose to become. In this particular case *you* chose to become who you are. You also chose to become what you are. You are not a victim of chance or circumstance. You are, however, stuck in a cycle of repeating what you have already done, and this cycle is what you are now trying to break.

You are not who you believe you are, so stop punishing yourself with harsh thoughts for not being perfect. The perfection you seek is already yours. Once you can learn that you came into life to experience a particular role, you will lighten-up and enjoy your role. *You are here to be you!* You are not here to be other than human! You came into this particular life to *create*. It is not your place to judge. You are an artist, you are not a critic. You do not belong in fear and pain. You are causing fear and pain by blaming and judging. If you can just give up blame and judgment for a short time, you will begin to feel better. Blame does not feel good when it runs through you. You will find that judgment sticks to you like old gum sticks to hot pavement, and when you walk over it, it will stick to the bottom of your shoes and everything else you walk on. It will make a mess, and anyone can see where you have walked by following the path of sticky marks on the floor.

You are not here to be a judge! You are here to be human, and you are God in human form. You may believe that God hates you or does not love you. This has, in turn, caused you to hate you and not love you. You may believe you are not worthy and unlovable. You are worthy, and I am here to tell you that you certainly are lovable! You stopped loving you because you started to judge what you did not understand. Part of what you did not understand is the ability to do anything and the creative force that runs through you. You do not understand your own creative genius. You have put your own self down as being uncontrollable and dysfunctional when, in actuality, you are creating and experiencing life.

You are afraid to accept nature, and this creates many great fears for you. You *are* nature and so you try not to be, out of your fear of it. You will find that once you begin to understand how you are a part of creation, as well as a part of the creator, you will allow yourself the creative flow that you now block. Once the flow is blocked it backs up and creates overflows in other areas. There is no evil, there is no bad, there is only a blockage in the flow that is causing people to react in distinctive and thus dysfunctional ways. You are all doing this in one or more areas of your life. You all *learned* how to judge simply by being *in* judgment. Now is the time to come out of judgment. There are no villains or bad guys, and there are no victims or good guys. You must learn how *you* create good and bad. Then you will be able to *open* the flow once again, and the blocks and overflows will cease and everything will flow as it is meant to.

You are nature. You have ebbs and flows like all of nature. You are not above nature simply because you have the ability to observe nature. You are observing you. You are part of everything and everything is part of you. You are going to find that you feel better, and create less pain, once you give up blame. Blame is at the base of your pain, it sits next to judgment and they drive you like one drives the car. You are going to release judgment by seeing how bad you are or where you are blaming you for being you. Do not be upset with you when you begin to see where you are judging and blaming you. Do not try to shift this blame and judgment to your mate, lover, child, friend, enemy, or whomever. It is only you seeing how you do not accept you, so that you might *change* this cycle of un-acceptance you are stuck in.

You are coming out of blame, so it will feel like blame. Do not fear it. Do not judge it. Do not push it back down in you. You have cleared enough to be strong enough to accept your own blame in order to release it. You have a great fear of blame because you believe the blamed belong in jail, or in some form of punishment. This is not so; however, I do not wish to intrude on this strong belief at this moment. Just know that you will have a difficult time accepting blame because, in your past (all of your pasts), blame meant repercussions of some sort. You do not experience lifetime after lifetime of blame and repercussions without it having a strong effect on you. You have been programmed to *believe* "bad" is a punishable offense. Being bad is the *result* of accepting blame for something.

Do not fear blame if it leaves you. Know it for what it is and know also that, in clearing, what goes into the closet must eventually come back out. You are simply cleaning your closet and making room for light in your life.

$\mathcal{A}$s you begin to clear blame you will see it rise up in you. This is how you know it is leaving you. Do not be afraid to experience blame and do not be too hard on yourself as you feel self-blame and resentment. The greatest need within you will be to project your blame onto another. You do not wish to be the focus of blame, so you direct blame towards anyone else who will accept it, or is unable to reject it. You are not doing this to create a better environment, but simply to keep you safe. You see, along with blame you have self-punishment and the pain that it creates. You are afraid of pain, and so you ignore it and you shut it off at any cost. Most of you do not know how much pain you are in because you have diverted your pain into activities that occupy you and keep you busy. Pain is created as a signal, and emotional pain is just as great a signal as physical pain.

Your pain centers are blocked and out of balance from being shut down and ignored at any cost. You will find that in order to release your pain you may need a big charge, or painful situation, drawn to you in order to get pain 'within' moving up and out. This is also true of blame. In order to get blame moving up and out, you may draw a very big movement stimulator. This could be any kind of a situation that will trigger and start action for blame. Watch for situations in your life that cause you to panic. Panic is the big energy boost that often sets things in motion. Once panic has started to move you to action, you have enough adrenaline going in you to cause a great deal of movement. Normally you do not like the feeling of panic or fear, as you 'fear' fear so strongly. Once you come to understand how everything about you serves a purpose, you will no longer fear parts of you.

As you learn to allow your system 'within' to clear its old programming, you will become more and more comfortable within your own self. At this point there are many who do not feel comfortable within their own bodies, and therefore spend a great deal of time outside the body. For now we are working on cleaning the energy blocks out of you so you can feel comfortable "in" you. Once you get to the point where you feel comfortable "in" you, you will begin to feel comfortable in any situation. The only reason you do not accept certain life situations now is because you do not accept "you" now. Once you accept "you," you will begin to accept God. This occurs automatically with self acceptance. You are God; ergo self acceptance is God acceptance.

Now; you all know that God is the big head honcho right! So, once you accept God, you automatically accept all that God is. And what is God? God is "all that is." God is creator. God is "all that is." God creates "all that is." "You want it – you got it," that's the God option, or buyer's option when you buy into the fact that you are indeed the big guy.

So; what keeps you from being the big guy? Fear! Fear is what came between you and you. You split! You became two parts of the same whole. You left part of you as a way to fragment and become more, but what ultimately occurred is you became a mess instead. You created a process by which you stretched what you are until it was unrecognizable as "you" any longer. You then pointed at this "you" and decided, "This is my enemy." It is not your enemy; it is "you." When you can accept "you," you will no longer feel so hurt and split apart and alone. You will begin to know that you are love, and that you have great love, and that you give love, and that you receive love, and that love is what you have always searched for. You will finally have joy because you will have "you" back. You will have found the greatest love you could ever imagine inside of you. Your search will end. You will be fulfilled and you will know God once again.

Is it worth it to "move" your pain and is it worth it to move your blame? Do you want to continue to sit on it in a frozen lump of despair, or are you ready to give up your position and allow pain to move in you so it might be you? You will, of course, feel it when it moves and you will want to stay calm. I have just completed this project with my pen. She has cleared pain from the right side of her body and is now clearing from her left. It felt to her as though it were mild, other than a few months of twinges and fairly sharp pain that was not debilitating, but sometimes a little draining on her. It was not determined that she should suffer, but rather that she would assist pain as it left her. She is now clearing pain from her left side and, of course, she will feel much better once she has completed this "release" of old blocked energy in her.

It is not brutal to release pain. It is, however, uncomfortable and you will need to be patient. Most of Liane's pain left slowly and gradually with little discomfort. At the peak of her energy release, she was uncomfortable enough to take aspirin in order to feel well enough to continue her daily routine. Do not fear pain. Learn to work "with" it and allow it to move out of you. You may wish to assure it that you are not going to shove, or push it back down in you, as you have in the past. I know this does not sound attractive nor is it appealing to you, but it is one of the biggest blocks keeping you from your own self love and, consequently, from joy. I want you to have love and joy again. Do this work and you will. It is not evil to want you to clean out the psychic closets "within" you. It is evil (fear) to hold on to the separation that this block creates. If you choose to hold on to your pain you will not feel love; you will not feel joy.

Let go of your pain. Allow it to release and you will feel love and joy. They are trapped behind all the pain that you have taken "in," let the pain go "out." Give pain a passage by allowing it to be felt. Say, "I love you and I release you." It will hurt a lot less going out than it did coming in. You hold on to it as a way of reminding yourself to never let certain situations occur again. Now I am asking you to let it go. Some of you have great pain, be it emotional, mental or physical. Others have lesser degrees of pain, and you will each be frozen according to how much fear you have of the pain, as well as the situation that caused your pain. You will each "move" when you are ready. I just want you to know that it is possible and it is productive to "move" you and your pain. This will be a very big step for you, and you will reap all the rewards and benefits of being "free of pain."

As you grow in light you will begin to feel uncomfortable. You have lived in darkness for so long that you will want to return to what you know. You are most comfortable with what you know, and what you know appeals to you. You will find that you are very attached to the darkness out of your fear of the unknown. The unknown, at this point in your evolution, is light. You do not know the light of love, and it will feel strange and uncomfortable for you. You will find that you are being drawn *very slowly* into the light for just this reason. You have the ability to find something wrong with anything that you choose to. This allows you to "disgrace" yourself and others. Once you have disgraced yourself, you no longer believe that you are worthy or lovable. You become ashamed, and you blame yourself for whatever has occurred and started your feelings moving in this direction.

Most of you do not know the light because you do not like the light. It is more comfortable for you to hide in darkness than it is to be exposed to the healing light. Light will change you and light will allow pain to surface (and all other symptoms of illness and disease). Light is not so much being born as it is being let in. Light has not been allowed to enter certain areas and those areas remain unconscious. Once you are ready to regain consciousness, you will be ready for the light to turn on "in" you. Once you have a little light, you will begin to release your darkness. We all have darkness, and we all have the ability to release what we hold on to and allow the light to stream forward and envelop us.

As you begin to awaken to your own ability to turn on the light within you, you will also find your need to turn it off, so that you may continue as you always have – without any change in direction. Once the light has caught your attention it will be difficult to return to unconsciousness. It is possible to do so but quite difficult. You will be interested in the light because it is your original state of being. The darkness was evolved into, just as you evolved into being an adult. You feel as though it just happened to you, and now the light is going to just happen to you.

You will not know what has hit you at certain points in your evolution. You will look around and think, "How did I get here" and, "What happened to the old me," and most often you will wonder, "What is going to become of me?" This is all due to the fact that you are transforming from one energy flow to another. If your true self decides to take the high road and allow the light to take over, you will feel like something is pulling you or maybe dragging you along. Do not be afraid of this process. You are not dying in a literal sense, even though you may feel that you are.

As long as you become light, you will feel uncomfortable up until you become equal parts of light and dark. At the point of equal parts you may have great confusion and maybe even chaos. This point of equal mixture causes great disturbance, and it is literally the point of turning. You are experiencing a great turning point in the creation of you. You are feeling what you are inside, and you also feel the opposition created when consciousness begins to wake up the unconscious.

As you learn to adapt to each step along the path of awakening, you will become other than what you were. You are transforming into a being of light, and to be a being of light is what you desire, or you would not be clearing and releasing your darkness. To become a being of light is to become your true self. You are love and light, and you went unconscious so you could believe you were other than love and light. The path back to you is a long one in certain cases. Do not be afraid to take time to heal. Do not be afraid to take time to release the old and be born again in the new. The new, in this case, is actually the old since you were light long before you were dark.

Now; when you begin to transform into a light being, you will feel the old dark being dying. It is going. It is becoming light and, as it becomes light, the dark parts disappear. This causes trauma for you. You are aware of changes in you and you are afraid that you are falling apart. You are actually beginning your process of coming together, but, because you have been fragmented for so very long, this process of becoming whole will be most uncomfortable. Have heart and love you, and do not condemn you for taking the high road. You are loving you, and that is why you (higher self) have decided to become a light being instead of a dark shadow. You are stepping out of your disguise and you were becoming your true self. You are a light being and you do shine in grace.

~~~

Once you become accustomed to your own light, you will no longer feel discomfort, and clearing will become easier. You are in a very rare position here. You *know* what you are doing, and yet the part of you who claims ignorance and holds the old programming does not quite understand. This part of you, who is programmed from lifetime to lifetime to be less than God, will not want to become a light being. Why? Simply because it is programmed to believe that God belongs in heaven, far away and definitely not inside of you.

Once you begin the process of taking on light you begin to change who you are. This is the time you begin to see how you will struggle to stay the same old you and hold fast to your fears and beliefs and denials. Unfortunately you have not yet become light enough to simply transform in an instant. However, once enough of you have made this passage, you will begin to see others make it with less fuss and less struggle and less confusion. This is due to the fact that each of you is connected and, in a way, each of you is affected by every other one of you. You do not yet realized the extent of your connection to the whole of consciousness but, for now, you will focus on you and what is in you.

I do wish to explain for you how I exist in and out of you. You are part of God and God is very much a part of you. The problem lies in logistics and can be seen only as an "us or them" scenario at this time. The true scenario is probably more an "us and him" one, but for now we will focus on the truth you deal with, which is an "us and them" mentality. For the most part you are all one, and the one that you are took on a specific identity that we will call human. Now, this human identity has specific traits and these traits often mark the evolution of this particular identity. One of the ways to identify a human is by its ability to stand erect and to speak. Not all who stand erect are human and not all who speak are human. This, however, narrows the field down a bit and we have less to sift through when looking for our human identity.

So, once you are born, you become human. In some cases, if you are born deaf and dumb and therefore cannot speak, you feel left out like you do not fit in. In other cases, if you are born without the use of your legs, you also feel left out and do not feel like you fit in. These are two very big signs or identifying ways in which we create and live as humans. So, if you begin with these two identifying marks of the human species, you will certainly not cast out those who cannot speak or walk, as nonhuman. They are indeed human; they simply do not have the required identifying marks.

Now; when you first entered your body, you believed you must have certain traits or identifying marks in order to be labeled "human." One of these identifying marks is aging. If you came into a body that never aged, you would not have "matured" in the womb to become nine months old and ready to enter the world. Also, if you did not age you would not grow from nine months to an age suitable for walking and talking. After all, growing up is part of the human condition. I don't think anyone would want to stay at the diaper stage for an entire life. And how about being stuck at age six for an entire life? Or maybe age thirteen with all those hormones running through your body? How can you want to stop aging when you created it in order to evolve to the next level? It is not a sign of death in a destructive way.

Aging is the natural process that you decided you wanted to experience. It is like wanting to be a flower. You know it will go through various stages of development and then it will wilt and wither away. Your options in the beginning were to not wilt and wither away. You could simply evolve to a rose and be stuck in the full bloom stage of evolution and not go anywhere from there. You chose to continue to evolve and to pass from the third dimension and go into other dimensions. Now you are afraid to pass from this dimension, and you desperately want to be frozen in time at one age or another. Trust me when I tell you that you have tried this and did not find it very fulfilling. You froze yourselves at specific times and the repetition was most un-valuable for your evolution. So now you evolve to maturity and beyond maturity to other levels of enlightenment. Only here on earth do you fear death and aging so. Once you move on to other dimensions you are very happy to be there. From here it looks like you end, but you do not end, you go on.

Now; aging fears are brought about by the lack of love within you for you. You do not love you and so you fear being you. Once you turn on your love light you will begin to love you, and you will gladly accept all phases of your evolution. Aging does not mean becoming wrinkled and ugly. You decide in your own mind to call silver hair ugly and sagging skin ugly. You do not mind baggy clothes that are not so tight and restrictive, so why do you mind skin that becomes more pliable and comfortable with age. You grow into you and you grow out of you, it is as simple as that. You do not stay you forever and for that you should be very grateful. "You," this you sitting here, is about as big as a point, or speck of dust, that is visible only by the strongest microscope available. There is so little "you" in this speck that you almost do not exist. You are, however, connected to the very big grandness that is the whole you.

So, do not be upset about gray hair and wrinkles. God does not make you look like this to give you a complex. God does what is creative. This is a very good creative way of showing you how wise you are and how evolved you are. You will learn to equate age with beauty when you decide it is okay to grow old and evolve. As long as you are stuck in youth and tight skin you will not accept evolution. You will accept fear of moving forward, which may cause other fears and phobias to form. Love your age whatever age you are, and thank God that you do not fit in one stage of your evolution for eternity like a marble statue. You get to move and grow and flow from one dimension to the next. You have no idea what you would miss, and how much you would miss not moving forward. To be stagnant is not your wish. You like to move and flow with creative energy.

You go to a very good place when you leave earth. How can you have forgotten so much? How can you not remember how beautiful it is? Oh yes, I remember now. You were programmed to forget where you came from so you could enjoy your stay here on earth.

≈❧≈

*W*hen you become light, you literally become energy. Light produces its own energy and it will allow you to create greater light within you. When you first begin to transform, your light will be small and it will be forced to stay small until it can grow enough strength to push upward, just as you might see a flame do. If you light a candle it may start to flicker until the flame gets big enough to hold its own. Then it will begin to grow into a steady glow and it will be strong. After you pass the initial stages of being turned-on, you will begin to take over the rest of you. The light will gradually consume any darkness within you. When this occurs, the residue from the darkness will begin to surface and you may feel quite burned out and exhausted from it.

You are just now beginning transformation, and you will do most of your healing in a slow and progressive manner. You will not be put off by your burnout and you will continue to clear and release residue from within. This is an important time for you, and it will allow you to transform into the light and to continue to live in this state of ascended grace. You will find that you are being changed willfully and not un-willfully. Your full acceptance of this process has brought you to this point in your evolution. You (higher self) know exactly what you are doing and you realize how you are changing and growing. You are not being forced into this process of transforming to light. It is the plan. It is your plan. You are the one who benefits from changing, and you are the one who rises up in this process.

Before you entered earth you decided to change a few things. Mostly, you decided to be more God-like and less evil. This is done simply by changing your attitude in regards to what God is and what evil is. These attitudes are buried deep in you and have existed through many cycles and many lifetimes. You are learning how to change what you are by changing what you believe. You are what you believe, and so to change the belief is the key to changing what you are. You may begin to change on a whim, or you may request change out of a desire to escape pain, torment and confusion caused by all that you currently believe you are.

Once you begin to change your beliefs, you begin to create a *shift* within you that will allow room for light to grow. This light then begins small, and steadily dissolves fear or darkness away. Each fear will hold on to you out of a need to survive, and you will hold on to your fears out of a belief that they are *right* and *just*. You will begin a struggle that will end in your fear leaving and the light taking over. You will go through ups and downs during a big release, or letting go, of fear. This will end with some panic or maybe sorrow at loss. The loss is, of course, the fear that has just been lost to the light. In a similar manner you were transformed from light into darkness. You dissolved into darkness and now you are reversing that process. For many of you, this is your singular purpose in this particular lifetime.

You are here at this time to transform in great numbers. It is not only you who is going through this process, and not everyone realizes what is happening inside of them as they transform. It is not a process that is consciously discussed, but it is known about on an unconscious level and it will continue for some time. Eventually this process will become easier as more and more of you transform to light and begin to feel "grace." You will affect the others and they too will begin this process, and since the first team has brought in so much light it will not be such a struggle for the second group. You will find that this entire process will take maybe ten earth years and then you will begin a new phase which will be an "adjustment" to the light. After adjustment you will feel a "blending" of sorts, where the light in you connects with the light in others and you "feel" the connection of one with another, and you know that you are all God or one Creative Force.

This is pretty much the path you are walking. If you find yourself reading this page in this book, you have been led to this point for a reason. Use what you are learning to inspire yourself and to show gratitude to yourself for having chosen this path. You are not really falling apart, you are losing big parts of you that were dark and it feels like you are falling apart. Let yourself go through this process. It will allow you to become "more." More is what you are. You think you are so small because you do not "feel" the rest of you. You are actually quite magnificent, you are brilliant! You are so bright that you outshine any star. You simply have not become *aware* of this part of you.

The gift you gave yourself this particular life was the gift of transforming from one energy form to another. You are all walking this path, and some may arrive at the point of change sooner than others. This does not matter, for all must eventually grow, and to grow is to become light. It is impossible to remain a seed or even a tiny sprout forever, unless you are solid marble or maybe a painting. For those who are alive, you will grow, and you will at some point begin transformation. It is what you came here to earth to do. You are here to assist God as he/she is born into the earth. God has come into his/her creation and creation is assisting. This is the time, this is the place and you are the chosen ones... all of you!

∾⊷⊶∾

Once you begin to take on huge amounts of light, you will clear huge amounts of darkness. The bigger the light, the bigger the amount of darkness you can move at one time. A tiny pinpoint of light is only going to move small amounts of dried up or blocked energy in you. You need a good healthy piece of light to move a good healthy chunk of darkness. So; for some time you will gradually, and oh so slowly, move darkness in you. Once you take on a larger portion of light, you will move things up and out a little faster and with greater momentum. You still will not like it when your darkness (fear) surfaces, but you will be able to deal with it very quickly considering the amount of the light you have taken on.

Most of you do not know how to begin this process so you do not know how to stop it either. It is not stoppable, simply because it is a part of creation and it was originally created to allow you freedom. Freedom from pain is what you are after. Freedom from pain is what you desire. Desire gets the ball rolling, and before you know it you are being forced to clear. You believe that God is forcing you to deal with life and struggle. It is not God. It is your own "desire" to rise above pain. You may accuse God of giving you burdens to bear, but it is really "you" creating an outlet for the cause of your burdens. Certain beliefs and thoughts that are "held in" you may cause certain behaviors "in you," which in turn may cause certain situations to become part of your existence. If you want to change, you will know it. You will feel a need to eliminate pain and suffering from your life.

At this point in your creation you do not realize how you *are* creation and you *are* creator. Once you begin to see how you are both creator and creation, you will allow yourself to continue what you have started. Part of you knows how you are set up and how you work. That part of you, that remembers who and what you really are, will allow you to continue to clear darkness, because that part of you does not fear "light." That part of you does not fear being God! That part of you does not fear! That part of you *knows* that the darkness does not really exist, and that part of you has created a way out of the darkness for you. It (higher self) has created a way to work within the parameters of your narrow belief system in order to bring you out of an imagined hell. You are not really in hell or darkness.

You have been programmed to believe you are and so you see what you believe.

Once we teach you how to overcome what you think you see, you will no longer fear being you and you will realize that creative energy is only a way to create, and anything that is created can be uncreated. You can learn how to create and un-create at will, once you take on enough light to "clear" out the majority of illusionary darkness that you "believe" you are. Once you carry your light into all parts of you, you begin to heal all parts of you and to use all parts of you. There are many areas in you that do not get touched by light, only because you have unconsciously blocked off those areas in an effort to avoid what you did not want to see or feel.

As you shed light on these areas they will be sensitive to the light and it will cause discomfort. If you took a prisoner out of the dark recesses of the cave that has imprisoned him for centuries, you would not guide him directly into bright sunlight. His skin would burn and his eyes would hurt. You need to allow a little light at a time, until he first can tolerate light. Then he must learn to accept light, and then he will gradually become accustomed to light enough to spend several minutes in bright light. As he builds his tolerance and acceptance of the light, he will be capable of spending more and more time in the light. You do not simply rush from living in the dark (illusion or not) to living in the light (which is your true state).

So; be kind with you. Be gentle with you. Do not push you and do not judge you. You are in a very gradual process, and each step has been carefully assessed in order to allow you the greatest comfort during this break with what you were, in order to allow you to become something much grander. You are not bad! You have been taught that you are sinful! You have much to change and let go of. Allow this process to take place. You will be so much better for it!

❧❧❧

*A*s you become more and more 'light,' your hold on darkness will slip away. This allows your hold on control to slip away. You will no longer feel the need to control everything, because you no longer feel the need to protect yourself from harm. You will at last know that there is no undercover agenda and the world is safe and it is okay to trust. Once you begin to take on the role of trust, you will begin to feel free and unrestricted or, as you might put it, "not so uptight." Once you have allowed yourself to relax, you will begin to unwind and this will allow your nerves to relax. You will no longer suffer from tension headaches and back aches brought on by tension. You will be relaxed and calm, and this calmness will bring comfort, and this comfort will bring joy.

Once you release your hold on control, you will allow yourself to let go of pain. For the most part, pain is now used by you to control you. You use pain to keep you in line just as your parents may have done with you as a child. You are hit or screamed at and it is painful, so you behave in order to not be hit and screamed at again. This is pain training. This is where you learn to punish you. You may have lived hundreds or, in some cases, thousands of lifetimes; and in any lifetime where you were hit or screamed at as a child, you learned how to exercise control by using pain and punishment.

You will not fully realize all the ways in which you control you, and thereby control your world, for some time yet. You will, however, begin to lose your hold on control, and this will allow you to relax and stop creating so much pain in your life. A great deal of pain is involved in your need to be free of pain. You seem to create more pain by your efforts to "avoid pain at all costs." One of these situations is your desire to stop pain immediately by taking a pill. This medication often creates its own side effects and problems. Another way, in which you create added pain by your desire to avoid pain, is how you treat one another in such a mistrusting way. This has caused a great deal of pain within your relationships, and it is one of the main reasons you now carry so much emotional pain.

It is not my intent to convince you in one instant to change and let go of all that you are and to release all of your programming in a day. No, I allow you the time you need to gradually let go of each teaching and to replace each teaching with a new, light teaching. You may not want to take this time to heal, but it is why you are here and it is not going to be so long and drawn out that you suffer unduly. You will begin to release gradually and you will become light gradually. Once you have taken on a great deal of light, you may begin to see how you are changing in big ways.

It is not so hard to allow yourself the time to change. You will feel a little better after each change and this will keep you on track. Once you let go of your need to control yourself, you will automatically stop trying to control others. Then you will really feel good. All that energy was going out to move and mold others, and now it will stay in you and you will feel more energy, or more of you will remain in you. This allows you to create at a very powerful level. Now, instead of creating small doses of good for yourself, you will be capable of creating larger doses of good for yourself. At some point you will begin to feel like everything is going your way, and you will begin to enjoy life for the simple fact that you exist.

Now; as you learn to direct your energy within rather than without, you automatically stop playing good guy/bad guy. You will automatically begin to see how everything is simply a created force that came from the creative force. Once you learn to let go of your need to control by releasing your control on yourself, you will begin to see miracles in your life every day. You will love life because you will be loving you instead of punishing you. You will embrace life as you have never before, and this will be due to the fact that you are embracing you. As you learn to be "in you," you will learn to be "in the world." Many of you are not in you, and therefore you do not feel part of the world. This, in part, is due to the avoidance of many parts of yourself. You are trying to avoid you, and so you do not trust you enough to come fully into the body, and you feel like you do not fit into the world. This will change. You will meld together and you will become whole.

❦

Once you begin to understand how you are simply programmed to be one way or another, you will be able to allow yourself to let go of old programming in order to enjoy your own self more than you now do. Most of you do not believe you have this powerful type of manipulation going on inside of you. You may "see" how others cause problems for themselves by repeating patterns, but you fail to "see" how you may create patterns that are repetitive and problematic for your own self. As you grow in light, you will begin to see how you are all right and okay whether you repeat troublesome patterns or not. You will learn how to accept yourself as you are. And then you will have the wisdom to change anything that you feel is not working to your own evolutionary advantage.

Here is the catch! No matter what you do – it is working to your evolutionary advantage. You just have such a big need to judge you as bad that you cannot, at this time, judge you as good. Taking on light will change things for you. You will begin to give yourself a break, and you will begin to allow you to be who you are without tearing yourself to pieces every time you "think" you are bad, or stupid, or wrong. You will begin to love you enough to allow you to take on many roles and not be so small and limited in who you are. This will allow you to become very adaptable to any situation that may occur. Adaptability is a great gift, especially if you live out in nature or if you are part of nature. As we all know, nature takes her own course, and if you can allow nature to take her own course, you can allow yourself (the part of nature that is you) to take your own course.

So; be free by allowing light to enter into darkness. This means you "allow" your programming to be destroyed and you "allow" something new to grow and take its place. This is how you will heal. You will heal by "allowing," and by knowing that you are good no matter what your feelings (which are connected directly to your programming) may tell you. You are good! You are innocent! You are loved! Now; I wish you to write these three affirmations every day until such time comes that you know deep inside of you that absolutely everything you do, say, feel, think, see or hear is good. Then and only then may you stop writing these affirmations.

Once you begin to see how you are the one who makes you miserable by the way you perceive reality, you will begin to perceive reality in a whole new way. You will begin to allow reality to "be" and you will begin to allow you to "be." You will stop your constant need to protect you by changing everything outside of you. Once you begin to "accept" reality you may then "shift" your perception of it. Once you shift your perception of it you can use it to your advantage. None of you know how to deal with your own power to create, and this causes problems for you. With "light" you learn how to create within the flow, without struggling to change the flow. You will let it occur and ride with it instead of fighting against it.

You sometimes exhaust yourself in the fight to gain control over a situation. You need not struggle; you may simply "let it go." One of the most powerful things you can do in any given situation is to "let it go." Do not judge it, and allow it to be. Then you have acknowledged that it has a force of its own and you are going to work within that force, or maybe around that force, but you are not going to drain yourself by pushing directly against that force. Once you learn to use energy wisely, you will appreciate reality a whole lot more than you now do. You will also appreciate the fact that you are part of this game of reality, and you will know how to work "in" reality as opposed to working "against" reality.

So; learn to take on light so that you might become part of creation in a whole new way. This is man's opportunity to become creator and to know on a conscious level that creation is positive and does not have to be negative. No matter what you see, allow it to be okay even if you cannot label it as good. It will later be acceptable to you, but for now, we must work with you where you are. Look for the good! It is always there and you can find it if you try.

You will begin to feel best when you are slipping back into your old, comfortable ways. This is where you are most at home until you can take on enough light to feel comfortable in the light. Most of you begin to change, and right away you start to feel like a new person and so you stop changing and stay right where you are. You do not get more than a step or two in the new direction but, for you, it may feel like huge progress is made. Once you become more accustomed to being "in" change, you will no longer feel so insecure with change. Change is a growing energy and it must be allowed to take hold of you gradually. You are too easily hurt by your own beliefs. And so to move you quickly allows you to judge and hurt yourself more than necessary.

This process of transformation takes time for a reason. Actually, it takes time for many reasons. You will find that, not only do you benefit from moving slowly into change, you also benefit from not being instantly transformed. Most of you would love to be simply "zapped" into a new you. This is not possible at this time for many reasons. One of which is the shock it would create within your consciousness. You would need another ten to twelve lifetimes on earth just to recuperate from such an extreme measure. You will, however, be able to zap yourself into new states of being once you have taken on enough light.

You have always been in one process or another, and this one lifetime is simply a process, or the process of this particular moment. Once you allow yourself to become light, you will move on to the next process. One of your problems is that you want this process to end. You do not end, not ever. You think you can find an end to things by ending your life but that does not end "you." "You" continue and "you" go on forever! You will continue to evolve until you get to the next level. And once you reach the next level you will continue on to the next, and then the next, and the next, and so on and so forth. "How long" is, of course, your first question and your answer is – "forever." You do not always struggle on your path to ascension. It is only here that you are ignorant to energy, and how it is you, and how you use it, and how it is making you whole.

Once you get beyond this original step of converting what you once were into a new form, you will find hope, faith, trust, pleasure, joy and love. These are your gifts and they have always been right here "in" you. Some of you felt them strongly before you began your process of transformation, and they allowed you to move into this process with great hope and trust and faith and pleasure and joy, and most of all love. You experienced a little of what it would be like to uncover these virtues in yourself, and it felt so good to feel them that you dove right "in" to the experience of transformation and change. Now you are a little bogged down by the weight of your emotional and psychological debris. This causes you to question and to look for new answers. This too is simply part of this process.

Once you become more light than dark, this whole process will move much faster. You will find that you move through what you call the bad feelings much more quickly, and you receive your answers much more quickly. This will continue until you are literally making changes in you in a blink of an eye. You will move through old buried feeling in the wink of an eye, and your discomfort will be over in a matter of seconds if not minutes. You will receive so much for your efforts because you have so much "in" you.

Once you get the buried hurt up and out, you will find your pleasure behind it. Once you get your feelings of doom up and out, you will find your hope behind it. And once you get your feelings of hatred up out, you will find love behind them. You are not going to like clearing and releasing these emotions, but you are going to enjoy the results of your labor. You are going to feel great again. As a matter of fact you will feel better than you have ever felt in your life... in many lives!

Once you have taken on enough light, you will become very independent and wise. You will no longer look to others for validation or love. You will be validating and loving you to such an extent that the overflow will go from you outward. You will no longer feel the need for acceptance, and you will be very, very tolerant of any given situation or event. You will know true wisdom and with wisdom comes joy.

Wisdom is enlightenment, and enlightenment allows you to be in the light at all times. Emptying you of darkness and old programming is the first step to enlightenment. Do not be upset with you for clearing out your garbage and debris. You are doing a good thing by doing so. And do not be upset with you when the garbage and debris come to the surface and "create" situations as they leave. Everything has energy and energy moves and creates. Do not be upset by anything that may be drawn to you as a result of clearing old, blocked energy. Like attracts like and you may attract exactly what you are releasing. Do not fear. You are not being bad, you are simply clearing, and clearing is a good thing!

When you become light, you will be totally free to express yourself without fear of recrimination or rejection. You will no longer be afraid to be wrong because you will no longer believe in wrong. You will actually begin to like who you are, and you will actually begin to like who everyone else is. You will no longer find differences frightening, and you will "feel" how you are all connected and, therefore, all one.

As you learn to adjust to the light, you may feel certain aches and pains. This will, of course, be in the beginning phase of clearing a specific problem or blocked energy pattern. As you release this energy pattern it may move slowly within you, and it may cause your aches and pains to move around also. Do not be alarmed if you feel neck pain or back and shoulder pain during a clearing. These areas are most affected due to spinal release. Your spine holds your body together, and it is connected to everything else in you. It is very common to clear through the spine then through the adrenals. You will find that your body will feel worse during a clearing and then better after a clearing. For the most part, you will not like clearing until you have released enough darkness and debris to begin to see how clearing blocked energy really does assist you, and make you feel better in the long run.

So; as you continue to clear away the old patterns, habits, problems, fears, emotional pains, bad thoughts and torment from childhood, and just general baggage that you carry, I want you to know that you are being productive, you are serving your purpose and you are being rewarded for your efforts. Do not fear that you will never feel better, because you will. It is not only better that you will feel, it is better than ever! You will begin to take to life like a duck takes to water. You will become open to life and this will allow you to become open to who you are. You will no longer close down. You will have reversed your process of shutting-down into a process of opening-up. You will no longer shut out light, you will open to light. You will no longer shut out love, you will open to it. You will no longer shut out God, you will open to him.

You are re-creating you in order to allow you to evolve and to ascend to a whole new level. At this point in your creation, this does not happen in the blink of an eye. It occurs over a slow, methodical, stretch of time. During this stretch of time you may begin to feel as though your clearing will never end, but it is important for you to realize that it took a lot of years, and sometimes a lot of lifetimes, to accumulate a pattern large enough to block energy and to stifle you. You must accept that it will take a little time to reverse the patterns and release the flow once again.

There is also the problem of not remembering how it feels to be balanced. You know very well how it feels to be out of balance, and that is the most comfortable feeling for you. Once you can accept how it feels to be in balance, you will be capable of staying in balance for longer periods of time. As this continues, you will gradually regain your equilibrium, and you will then be able to maintain a steady flow of light within you. These are your conditions, and you have created them by your need for light. You have created what you do not feel comfortable with because you know that you have swung too far to one side and you must now return to center. For most of you it will not be long before you feel some benefits. You will begin to feel a new inner strength that has not been present in your life for eons.

Once you have experienced even a small amount of light, you will hunger for more. This hunger turns into a strong desire that begins to push you into yourself, simply because you contain the light you so desperately desire. Once "in" you, you will begin to focus on all the areas that are blocking light by casting a shadow. If you can look into the shadow part of you, you can cast light on that part, and that part will then be forced to the surface and will no longer draw more darkness to it.

As you learn how to balance yourself you will begin to feel free of restriction, and the rules you have always lived by will fall away. This can be hard for you to accept if your rules have been your "protection" in a way that is not necessary. Some of you became perfectionists in order to survive, and it will be very hard for you to give up your perfect ways. It will feel like chaos to give up even a little bit of perfectionism. To let your hair blow in the wind, or to untidy your room or home may feel like you are turning into a slob. It is all relative to how strongly you need protection and how out of balance you are. Going in the other direction – if you require chaos in order to hide, you will have a difficult time accepting any amount of order in your life. Chaos represents freedom to you and you will not feel good about being orderly. It will feel like you are being controlled and choked to death.

Chaos and order meet somewhere in the middle, and the middle is where you are headed. When you get to the center of you, you will be able to make anything happen for yourself, and you will be able to be anyone you wish to be. The middle contains the source. To be centered is best!

≈≋

*W*hen you learn how to clear in an instant, you will be further into yourself than you now are. It takes some time to become fully conscious, and it takes some time to begin to realize how you are and what you are. Most of you are not altogether in you, and you do not believe that you are not in you. This, in itself, presents certain obstacles and prevents instant transformation. Fragmentation is the process by which you left parts of you behind as you grew up. This process was of major importance if you were abused as a child. The more trauma you experience, the greater your need to split off or fragment parts of yourself.

You are more split than you realize, and it will take some time to reclaim parts which were left behind. Often, these parts contained memories that are considered by you to be bad. If you return to a traumatic event in your past by remembering it, you often bring up the bad feelings attached to it. Therefore, you choose to forget and not remember. This is all taken care of in the subconscious mind, and it is often not in your current awareness. If you think there are things which occurred in your past and are now hidden from you consciously, then I suggest that you are more than likely split or fragmented. One way to tell is to be hypnotized and go into any traumatic event. Do not specify "this lifetime" and see where you go. If you begin to bring up memories of pain or trauma you are more than likely fragmenting.

So; if you wish to transform, it is a good idea to allow the time that it takes. I know how you hate to waste time on anything that does not give you immediate gratification, but this too shall change. You will learn to appreciate the job that time has and the benefits of time passing. You created time for a purpose and it served its purpose well. As you continue to let go of your undesirable feelings, you will benefit. This will take time! Each trauma in your life (be it this lifetime or another), has undesirable feelings attached to it or it would not be considered trauma. You are about to uncover who you are and you may not like all that is stored in you. Allow your feelings of inadequacy and unimportance and insignificance and unworthiness to surface. You will not die from "feeling." You will however be uncomfortable "feeling" these feelings, or you would not have buried them in the first place.

Anything that is buried in you is buried because you did not like it. Usually you do not like what does not feel good. So, I come along and tell you to "feel" what you do not like and, in doing so, you will ultimately feel good. You, of course, cannot understand how or why God would want you to feel something that feels bad, so you have a problem accepting that I am really God.

So; should God simply leave you to "hold in" all your pain and trauma and simply discuss flowers and pretty rainbows, or should God get right to the heart of your problem and explain to you that you no longer know how to love one another because you are so full of feelings that you dislike; and what you are full of makes you up, so you are made up of bad feelings to the extent that you can no longer "accept" you, because of course, you cannot accept bad feelings? So do you think God is punishing you by leading you into your bad feelings, or do you think that God is showing you the way out of bad feelings, by allowing you to decide to release them, by letting them come up in you in order to exit you? You will find that God does not enjoy your pain and suffering, and God only wants to show you the illusion of it all.

You feel bad about something that occurred many lifetimes ago and it causes you to feel bad today. Why? Simply because it is "in you." It is part of you. You, however, have the power to let it go by facing those feelings once again, and deciding you do not need to hold on to them as a way of protecting yourself from never being hurt again.

As you let go of your hold on bad feelings, you will allow them to come up in your consciousness and you will allow them to be *felt*. Do not be upset if you begin to feel bad. It is simply your bad feelings coming up to clear. You will feel moments of total freedom after you clear big traumatic feelings. You may feel a little like a crazy person since you will be releasing old traumatic feelings and, at the same time, you will know that this process is healing you, so your hope for a bright future will be evident. This is how you will feel most often. There will be times for some of you when you lose touch with those hopeful feelings, but they are still in you because some part of you *knows* that you are simply transforming.

※

*A*s you contribute to your own ability to ascend, you will begin to see how you do own you. You will once again know that you are not a victim of life and you will begin to feel powerful. Ignorance is based on not knowing. Intelligence is based on the ability and capacity to know. When you are in a state of knowing, you feel less frightened and more secure. When you are in a state of not knowing, you are very uncomfortable and quite frightened.

So; I have written these books so that you might know and be less confused. The biggest obstacle for you on earth is the dense field of matter. Matter allows for very little light at this time. Matter is changing and evolving, and as it does so your scientists will be quite astonished to find new agents in their world of physics. This is just part of God coming into all of creation. It is not that God consciousness is not already in every particle, it is more that God is fully forming or being born out of what God created.

Think of a world without procreation. No one is born to anyone. Then, at a specific point in evolution, one child is mysteriously born; then another child is born and soon another until everyone is bearing fruit. You are in the process of changing the molecular structure of your body so that you might bear fruit. The fruit that you bear is God. You do not know how this is possible because no one has borne fruit before. You are in a situation of trust, whereby you must begin to act as if you know what is going on in order to "assist" what is occurring. You are part of the process and you are the process. You assist and you allow the creation of an entire new way of living.

This new way of living is a way of creating heaven on earth. You are baking the first cake, and believe me when I tell you that it will taste like nothing you have ever experienced since you left the God force.

It will be miraculous to see you sitting there in heaven, when for so many lifetimes you have been confined to hell. To be in total surrender and to *know* God will give you such pleasure. You will literally become angels once again. Your joy will be so great that you will not ever fear anything again. You will come and go from earth without pain, and you will *know* that you are God.

As you evolve into this state of grace, you will no longer feel the need to fight or scream or argue or defend. You will simply *be,* and to *be* is very much what you are. As you begin to simply *be,* you will want to take your light with you. You are growing in light, and this light that is growing in you will allow you to sense joy, and it will also allow you to feel total love and acceptance of the self. This in turn allows you to feel total and complete love and acceptance of absolutely everyone. You will no longer need! Your "need" for anything will end, simply because your every whim will be met and satisfied by your ability to create light. Your creation of light is a very big gift to you from God. You are beginning to become what you are creating. You are coming into you and you are growing "in" you every day.

As you continue to grow, you will develop new attitudes and new ways to see everything. You will not always want to be stagnant and so you will begin to move. You will first begin to move from one place to another just to show yourself that you are not afraid to move. Then, once you have gotten used to the idea of movement, you will begin to cross dimensions. This is actually nothing new to you since you cross dimensions now, but it will be new to do it consciously and to "know" that you do it.

After you begin to move freely among the various levels of consciousness, you will then begin to move back and forth between you and God. You will be like a heart. You will be God one beat and yourself the next. You will "know" God and you will know that you are God. You will begin to cover more space very quickly, and you will soon realize how you are "connected" to God and then you will see how you are an extension of God. This will lead to the observation that it is all you! You are God Being and God Being is you. You will realize the full extent of your ability to create absolutely anything and then you will *know* how you created everything. You will feel this awareness and then you will become this awareness. This is the process by which you are being born.

*O*nce you begin to see how you are simply being forced to give up old programming by your desire to become light, you will no longer blame God or anyone else for your uncomfortable feelings. You will begin to realize how you are moving into the light, and how this is not comfortable since you have only known darkness. Once you adjust to the light, you will no longer fight it and you will begin to accept it as part of you. Once you realize how you are coming into you, you will not fight it; you will begin to accept you. Once you realize how you are being born again you will no longer fight it, you will accept it. You are the one who wants it and you are the one who came here to *experience* it.

As you learn to accept who you are you will begin to love who you are. You will become attached to this new you and you will cherish her/him, and you will know that your desire to take on light has been the creative motivation that moved you from the darkness out into the light. You will no longer hide parts of you simply because there will be nothing to hide. All parts of you will be acceptable, which in turn allows them to be lovable to you. You will no longer reject or deny any part of you. Cosmetic surgery will not be so popular and everyone will regain normal balance. No one will be obese simply because everyone will be accepting themselves and no longer rejecting the self. When you reject parts of you, you begin to push away parts of you.

This causes you to feel pain. You take on added weight to "protect" you. You need padding from this assault on you.

You will find that once you take on light, you will no longer "harm" you in any way. You will begin to see how you have used self punishment to control you, and you will give up this practice simply because you no longer feel the need to reject parts of you. You will, by acceptance of the light, be accepting you and you will, by acceptance of you, begin to transform. This is this process you are now in and there are many steps to this process. The most important step is to "allow" all that is occurring to simply "be." This is why I teach you to "go with the flow" and "do not judge." If you can live by these two mottos as you learn to accept all parts of you, you will not be sad or upset in any situation that may occur. If you can "go with the flow," you can be free of struggle, and if you can "not judge," you can be free of condemning and creating further need for pain through punishment.

Once you learn to take on light you will no longer fight with yourself at every turn. You will no longer judge you and this will allow you to be *free*. Freedom is your ticket out. Freedom means letting go of lifetime after lifetime of pain that was set in place by lifetime after lifetime of judgment, and lifetime after lifetime of condemnation. Once you let go of condemnation, you will let go of your heaven and hell theory and you will have only bliss. Heaven is awareness, and awareness can be found here and now. Hell is confusion based on ignorance, and hell can be found here and now. You can be in heaven here and now or you can choose hell. Either one is a choice and is based on either knowing and accepting, or refusing to know and rejecting. Allow everything to be okay and you allow yourself to be okay. Allow everything to be based on judgment and you allow you to be judged.

You set the creative force to action by your thoughts and your beliefs. These thoughts and beliefs are written on the pages of your mind, and then they are put to paper and brought forward for all to follow. Man began to think in ways that would assist his survival. One of his predominant thoughts was, "how can I keep from being hurt?" This thought was followed by another thought, "don't let anyone get close enough to hurt me." This thought was followed by, "how do I keep them away," which was followed by "build a big wall, have strong boundaries and enforce them with rules." These are all survival methods and you are now past that stage in your evolution. You are now into you, and once you come into you, you no longer require such primitive forms of protection.

This is so very hard for you. To let down your protective barrier is so hard for you to do. It keeps you in and others out. It keeps you safe from others but not safe from you. You are in there (behind the barriers) with you. You hurt you out of a need to punish the offender. You judge you as an offender, so now; here you sit inside of this barricade, and the one you are most afraid of, the one who judges you and punishes you is right there with you. You are fighting a losing battle! Come to terms with you! Allow you to be set free. Allow the walls of protection to fall and allow yourself the freedom you deserve. Do not hide behind a barricade that was meant to keep everyone else out. It only serves to hold you prisoner. You are not going to find your freedom behind walls of protection. You create everything that occurs in your life, so if you create punishment it will find you because you are wherever you are!

❦

Once you begin to transform, you will begin to see a difference in how you accept your own behavior. You will begin to notice how you ease up on your control of you, and how you become gentler within your own decision-making process when it comes to your choices. This in itself will feel uncomfortable to you. If you have been a control freak, you will not feel good letting yourself go with the flow. To flow is to be free of rules and restrictions. To control is to have set rules and force yourself into patterns in order to control yourself.

Now that you are transforming, you are letting go of your control. This is part of your discomfort because you learned long ago that true freedom lies in your ability to be a specific way. If you do not control you, how will you be right, or perfect, or better, or safe? It frightens you to think of these possibilities simply because your life has been based on control. You control what you eat to stay a certain weight. You control what you say in order to fit in. You control how you act in order to be accepted. You control how you think in order to not be judged as weird or crazy. You even control how you see the world in order to allow it to be acceptable to you. You control your children, your loved ones and your pets.

You teach everyone how to treat you and how much of any given behavior you will accept before you get upset. You all know how far you can push one another or to what extent you can be pushed. You do not accept more than what is acceptable to you, and this allows you to stay in safe territory, which is hidden behind your walls. You are terrified of exposure, and once transformation begins, your process of freedom begins. This process includes dropping your walls to allow you to be exposed, which in turn will allow you to be free of your need to hide. You can exhaust your entire spirit by using all of your life force to build walls of protection, or you may set your spirit free by allowing the old ways to dissolve into a new form of being.

Once you give up control, you are open to receive everything that is available to your soul. Your soul is in dire need of assistance, and it is sorely in need of love. Love allows the soul to thrive! Not love like you think – not romantic attachment. I'm talking about true love! The love one feels for God or for life. It is a reverence of sorts. It is a great respectful knowing that allows one to be exactly what one is. Self love is the only love, simply because you are the entire universe. Everything happens "within" you. Anything that you "perceive" as outside of you is simply a reflection of what is within. Many of you love your cars because you do not know how to love yourself. Others love their children and make their children oh so important, simply because they cannot love themselves. Still others love their jobs because they cannot love themselves. There are even those who love animals or the earth more than they love themselves.

Those who have a great desire to save others are reflecting the desire to save the self. In the same way, those who have a great desire to change others, have a great desire to change themselves and are simply projecting. Do you fit into any of these categories? Are you loving everyone but you? Are you accepting everything but you? Are you treating everyone with kid gloves while you beat you up emotionally?

Watch your mirrors. See what you are doing and how you spend your energy. If you have a great desire to help others it is considered very admirable in your society. It is also a sign, or signal to you, that you have a great desire to help you and this desire is not being met. You are acting out on others what you want to receive, in an effort to get others to give it to you so that you will not have to give it to yourself. You were not taught to give yourself love or anything else for that matter. You were taught that God loves you when you are good and to obey his laws, and you were taught by your parents that they are nice and receptive to you when you are good and do not break their laws.

Once you let go of control of you, you are afraid you will no longer be good and acceptable. This, of course, leads us back to where we started, which is – you not being comfortable during the process of transformation, because it causes you to let go of specifically programmed behavior that has always kept you under control and safe from God and parents. Your carefully controlled ways are about to leave you and you will not like it at first. Once you release enough charge from these old controls, you will be free to give them up on your own. The first few steps will be difficult and quite upsetting for you. You do not like to break your rules, especially if you were strongly punished as a child for breaking rules.

You will begin to see a major shift in how you relate to others once you have broken some of the control you now exert over yourself. You are growing in awareness in order to assist this process. What you know does not frighten you as much as what you do not know. You like to know what is going on in and around you, as it makes you more comfortable to know. To not know brings stress and anxiety. You prefer being aware and your new state of awareness has many benefits.

Many will remain unconscious while the first of you begin to wake up. Go about your life calmly and quietly in order to allow the others their need for sleep. You are not here to control others. You are not even here to control you. You are here to bring in light. You are doing what you came to do. Do not judge you for letting go of the rules and do not judge you for not being another. You are you for a reason. Actually, you chose everything about who and what you are. You were aware of your *entire* life when you chose to be you, so do not judge your decision. You knew a great deal more at the time than you now do.

So; love you and allow you to be who and what you are. Do not be afraid to let go of the old you even though the old you is the most comfortable place for you to be. You are moving into the light of love and the old you is most comfortable in fear and shadow.

∾❦∾

*D*o not be afraid when you begin to change! Some of you may go from a glamorous lifestyle to a not so glamorous one. Others may go from a very rigorous lifestyle to a very calm one. You may feel as though you have lost your edge in the consumer marketplace and, to a degree, you have. You are losing your sharpness and you are becoming soft and rounded. What was once very important to you may not be important to you now. You will more than likely "slow down." Your speed is directly related to your need to run from you or from specific life situations.

You may go from being an overachiever to being less than goal oriented. This will upset you if you have always been an overachiever. This is due to the fact that you *need* to be good or great at life in order to be accepted by you. You see, you decided that in order to be accepted it is necessary to achieve results in the world in a big way. It started out as your effort to please others and then it just became your effort to please yourself. Now, if you are not achieving a great deal in your life, you feel like you are not acceptable.

So; allow you to slow down if you will, and allow yourself to know that you are acceptable no matter what you do in life. You are not going to be admired and respected by all those higher-up management bosses, but you can be respected and admired by "you." You can allow you to slow down and not need praise, or adoration, or acceptance from others. You can be very, very happy by your own initiative to do so. You need not have the new cars and new homes and exotic vacations in order to feel good about yourself. You need not get rid of your big new car, or your lavish home, or skip those exotic vacations to the south of France. It is all just a symbol of what you *need* in order to feel acceptable. Those of you, who do not at this time live the lifestyle of the rich and famous, need not feel superior to them simply because you do not give yourself financial wealth.

Wealth is simply energy and energy blocks are all over "in" you. You can block the flow of anything into your life, simply by your ability to shut things out and keep you in and safe. If you do not have money it is because you do not know how to unblock your frozen energy. It has nothing to do with how deserving you are.

It has everything to do with how undeserving you believe you are.

In some cases you had remarkable wealth in another life and decided it caused you to behave in ways you did not like. Some of you become so paranoid when you have great fortune, and you believe that everyone is only interested in you because you have lots of it. In most cases you are right! If you are rich you are considered famous. Fame is part of being wanted and needed by others in order to feed their unfulfilled needs of being unacceptable. If you have a wealthy friend, you feel a little safer and more secure. Then, if that wealthy friend does not give you what you need in a time of trauma, you do not like them and you do not accept them in your life. This is friendship based on a need to meet one's own insecurity.

If you find that you do not have wealth and are constantly thinking of money, you are being afraid of lack or maybe you are feeling insecure. To open the flow, you must take on enough light to allow yourself to let go of your fear of lack and to allow yourself to know that you deserve. The easiest way to show yourself that you deserve is to love you and accept you. The only way to love you and accept you is to eliminate your internal blocks that keep you frozen in mistrust and imprisoned, by you, in you. You do not need to be a rocket scientist to realize that like attracts like. You do not need to be a genius to know that if you block-up you and build walls to keep everyone from getting at you, you will not be "free" to move "out" into the universal flow.

So; you are stuck, by you, in you! To un-stick you it is necessary to pull down the walls and get the frozen energy patterns moving. To move energy that has not moved in a very long time can be traumatic and frightening for you. This is mostly done at intervals so you can handle the level of fear that is to run up and out of these blocks. If you do not run the energy up and out, you push it down and in. This means you keep it, and it keeps growing in you until you can release it without harm to the psyche. You do not hold on to anything as tightly as you hold on to your fear of loss and lack of security. This is your biggest fear. Next is your fear of sexual energy, but that will be discussed later in other books. For now, I wish you to know that it is okay to let go of your need to be an over-achiever. You are loved and you are good and you are innocent. You have nothing to prove to anyone... not even to you!

❧

When you no longer see yourself as bad, you will begin to prosper. Prosperity comes when you let go of your bad feelings. This type of prosperity is, however, not what you think. True prosperity is of the soul. Soulful love is indeed very rare here in the third dimension. Soulful love is of the spirit and its rewards are of the spirit. Everything that you reach for is in an attempt to reconnect with the spirit. You believe that to love you is to be arrogant, and you believe that to trust you is to be foolish. Once you learn how valuable your connection to "you" is, you will no longer feel that you must put "you" down in order to control "you." You will begin to trust "you" and you will begin to allow "you" to "be."

Once "you" begin to "be," you will no longer feel like you are dysfunctional or that you don't function properly and must always be guarded. Once you let your guard down you will no longer feel tension as your body will be "at ease." Once your body is at ease, it will no longer create so many aches and pains and dis-ease in your life. Once you have let your guard down and made peace with yourself you will no longer find it necessary to "push" yourself, nor will you find it necessary to stimulate yourself with caffeine and sugar. You will be at peace, and this will be due to the fact that you simply put down your walls and let out your prisoner.

You all do this to some degree. You were all "trained" how to act from childhood on. Once you let go of your training you will become instinctual instead of programmed. From an instinctual perspective you will not harm another, simply because it does not have value. From an instinctual perspective, you will not be afraid unless you are actually in a threatening situation, such as a storm where the roof might blow away. You will not hide for the sake of hiding, and you will stop all the game-playing and role-playing and acting-out. No one will get hurt by you and you will not get hurt by anyone. This is trained behavior. It is not soulful love. It is something you were taught from early on. It is not your true nature to be violent. It is rage that causes you to act out. Rage held in is a very dangerous thing. It is most dangerous to the one who is locked in with it, and since you are locked up and held prisoner "in" you, you get to share space with rage. To be raged at day in and day out is very destructive to you.

You will find that as you learn to release your hold on you, you will begin to see how you can be wonderful without constant surveillance. You can be "you" without being "trained" or "programmed." You were 'you' long before your training. In an attempt to spare you pain and suffering, you were trained to act in specific ways to allow you to conform to society. This had a purpose but not a very practical one. Most of you are afraid of anyone who is different, so you cling together in groups and defend your right to be one way or another. You totally discard the odd guy who doesn't fit into a group.

Some groups learn to get along with other groups, but some never get along and fight generation after generation. You are programmed to take on the beliefs of your particular group. You may have been born into your group or you may have joined it voluntarily, but you will be "programmed" to maintain its rules and beliefs. This protects the group from falling prey to others and from collapse from sheer descent and dissension.

The one thing a group cannot provide for you is individualism. This is only obtained from within the self after learning to be the self. If you cannot be yourself, you cannot know yourself. This forming of society is not necessarily a bad thing. There were times when you all needed protection from vast numbers of huge, meat eating animals, and you fared better in life if you maintained a larger identity. Hence, you formed groups, and to this day you use your large body groups to demand a right and to right injustice. It served a purpose to form you into something you were not, but now it is time to go back to what you truly are. You are love and light. You need not continue to operate under the pressure and weight of an outdated belief system that says, "You are something that does not work properly and this is how you should work and behave."

You will find that as you learn to become who and what you truly are, it will feel wrong to you, simply because you have been trained to believe that "to be you is wrong and you must change in order to conform to the rest of society." It is very hard to move into a new direction when you are stuck in such a deep rut. This is the challenge of transformation and this is why it will be so disquieting for you.

You are not falling apart! The world, as you now live it, is. You are not dying, but the world that you have created in order to survive is. Your own little world is collapsing down around your ears, and you hate to lose it because you have lived there for so long. You are afraid to come in out of the rain simply because you have lived in it for so long. You are like a street person who will not leave the streets because of his or her own personal fears in his or her own head. I am telling you to come in and out of the rain. Do not be afraid to change. Do not be afraid to let go of old rules. Do not be afraid to be you. Be who you are, not who you were trained to be. Trust your feelings and your intuition. Let go of your fears and be free. Do not be afraid to be free. It is *safe* to be free!

*W*hen you begin to realize how often you are in confusion and use your defenses to assist you, you will begin to see how altered you are. As you uncover all of your fears, you will begin to see how you have always carried fear and have been altered by its presence in you. As you continue to release fear, you will be allowed to make your own way without the need to adjust "your way" (to accommodate your way of being in order to allow more space for fear).

You have adjusted you and you have stretched you as far as you can be stretched. Fear has taken up great space and now fear is leaving and you will feel "less" of you, only because a great part of you has always been full of fear. It is like weeding out a flower bed. Sometimes, when you take out all the weeds, you feel like there's not much greenery left in your flower bed. More of it was based on weeds than on flowers. This makes your flower bed appear to be barren and empty. When you weed out your life it too may appear to be barren and empty. This does not last for long. Once you remove all the weeds your flowers will have room to spread and grow. This will allow them to be bigger and fuller than ever before. Do not be afraid to weed out your life. If it is based on fear, then I suggest you pull it and toss it. If it is based on love of you, then I suggest you keep it and nurture it.

You will not be in a position to tell the difference between a weed and a flower for some time. Once you have taken on enough light, you will readily see how the weeds are very different from the flowers. After you have lost many weeds from your life, you may actually miss them. This is not because they gave you joy, it is simply because they gave you stimulation and you got used to being stimulated in such a manner. Humans have the ability to miss anything... even pain. So; if you find yourself not knowing what to do about losing things in your life, allow yourself the time it takes for new flowers to bloom, and this will add to your life and you will no longer be missing your weeds. It is not that you really miss weeds; it is more that you miss whatever is taken from you, even if it is a drug or cigarette.

Once you begin to see how you do not belong in pain, you will begin to ask for your pain to leave you. This pain is emotional as well as physical. Some of you have created a great deal of discomfort and dis-ease for yourselves by holding in your emotional pain. Your emotional pain accounts for a great deal of your physical pain. As you clear and release your emotional upsets and traumas, you are bound to clear and release the pain that is attached to them. This is simply part of the process of healing. It is not you being punished; it is you finding the courage to heal. It takes a great deal of courage for you to face your pain, and it takes a great deal of courage for you to face your emotions. You have been hiding from pain and emotions for a very long time.

Once you begin this process of releasing the emotions you will want to be patient. It took a long time to bind you up and now it will take some time to unbind you. It doesn't take as long to unbind you as it did to bind you, but it will seem long to you. You are very impatient, and you worry that you might miss out on life by taking time to focus on you and heal you. It is natural for you to feel this way since you are afraid of the passage of time. What if I told you that the only reason you are here on earth at this time is to unravel your pain, and release it here in this dimension where you first created it? What if I were to tell you that everything that you now create is created by your own knowing soul, in order to assist you in clearing your pain? What if I told you that you are not here to create big beautiful cities, but that you came here for the express purpose of letting go of pain?

What if I were to tell you that you (your soul) know exactly what it is doing every moment of every day? What if I told you that you feel (as a soul) that this is the most important work you can do for yourself and for humanity? What if I told you that you are not here to become rich and famous and look good to others? What if I told you that you (as a soul) are much bigger than the part of you who judges how you live, and that bigger part of you is here to release the energy that was picked up here?

What if I told you that the energy you brought back here has been infused with light and will assist others in releasing their energy? How would you feel if you knew that whatever you release and clear, in the form of pain, is held in you only by your will to hold it in? What if you knew that whatever you do you will continue to release pain until it is gone from you, simply because *your will* has decided to assist your soul? What if I told you that you are here to know "joy," and to know "joy" you must reduce pain? Pain and pleasure do not mix. You must release your pain in order to feel pleasure. Pleasure is the basis for bliss. Bliss is the true nature of you. You are actually a blissful being, and once you let go of your pain you will feel your bliss once again.

Originally you knew only bliss! You did not know pain. Now you know pain so well that to move you out of it may feel a little uncomfortable. Pain has become your common ground. You even tell painful stories and thrive on movies with heroes who tolerate huge amounts of pain. If you do not wish to see pain in your world, you must release the pain that you carry. You can only relate to another's pain by feeling your own pain. If you have a low threshold for pain it is simply because you are full. You are filled up with pain and can take no more. Some of you are so full of pain that you project nothing but pain. If you see a situation, you will automatically find pain in it because you are so full of pain that you are overflowing, and this overflow is projected out onto the world and you read pain into every little thing, simply because you are projecting and then looking at your own pain.

Pain is going to clear no matter how strongly you try to hold on to yours. It is meant to heal just as everything else is meant to heal. Do you know that you do not really fear death? What you really fear is the pain that you project onto death. If someone cuts their finger and makes a big deal out of it by screaming "it hurts, it hurts," you simply tell them to be brave and put a bandage on the finger. If someone is dying and screams "it hurts, it hurts," you get really upset, especially if you see them die. What you are doing is relating the death with "it hurts, it hurts." In actuality, death does not hurt! Death is a big release from pain. Actually death is a big release from "all" three-dimensional energy. So, do not judge death as painful, and do not project your pain and *your* dramas onto the rest of life. You are the creator of your reality and you get to believe whatever you want. For now try to believe that "everything has a good purpose" and "everything is good."

❧

*A*s you grow in the light you will begin to expand all that you are. To grow in light is to recapture your brilliance and to set all parts of you free. You have parts to you that you do not know. You have parts to you that act independently of your wishes. You have parts of you that believe it is their job to keep you in line by punishment and fear tactics. These parts learned early in life how to punish and how to frighten you. They learned by watching and listening. Once someone said "do not walk alone, you will get attacked," or "do not go out to play, you will get hurt," or "do not be so in a hurry or you'll have an accident," or "do not cry you'll lose all your fluids," or "do not cross your eyes, they may stay that way," or "do not trust anyone you do not know," or "do not receive anything from someone (the ones you can't trust) you do not know," you began to catch on. Part of you began its training in how to "help" you survive in this world. Part of you began to see how you would listen and respond to fear threats, and how you would be stopped dead in your tracks when punishment was also applied.

Part of being a child is learning how to be an adult. You emulate what you see and hear. You are being taught by those around you as to how you must "act" in order to be adult. To be adult is very important and quickly you are taught to be a big boy, or dad's little man, or mom's big helper. You are never, ever encouraged to act like a baby or to scream and act-out like a child. Always, the emphasis is on acting grown up. This creates a great deal of attention on your part, and so you learn to focus on and emulate the adults around you. You do this to the extent that some of you split off to become rather stern adults in a child's body. Actually you became split in the mind first. One part of you stayed in your child's state while another part took on the roles you were emulating.

These roles are part of you now. You have fears about getting hurt that have nothing to do with now and everything to do with what those you emulated feared the most. You picked up on their fears. You adopted their fears and you made them yours. They are not really yours and you may request that you become whole by recollecting all parts of you. This may cause your split and fragmented parts to return. You will draw them to you by your "desire" to own all of you. You will clear their pain by being patient enough to allow them time to release their pain. And you will, of course, feel their pain and there immense 'fear charge' because it, like everything else, is "in" you.

You will wish to know that, once you begin a spiritual journey, all parts of you are aware of exposure to the light and they may kick and fuss about coming out of hiding. After all, the only 'self' they know is the one that split and began to grow way back in childhood. They do not know another way, and they will need to emulate you now and your new way of seeing all that is.

You have an opportunity here to set parts of you free and to allow yourself to know all of you without fearing these parts of you. I have told you many times how you fear your own self as much as you fear God, who is also you. You will begin to feel what you are owning, and then you will know how you have been controlled by punishment and pain that has been dished out to you by some obscure part of you.

You hide parts of you from you and they have a purpose. Originally you taught them to emulate what you "thought" was important about being an adult. This determination was made because so much importance was placed on teaching you to fear punishment as a way to guide you and control you in childhood. After all; how many of you would tell a child to "go out and have fun, all is well and nothing can hurt you?" So you are threatened and punished in an effort to control your behavior and keep you safe. You now have adopted part of your parental zeal for punishment. This part of you does not hate you, this part thinks it is doing what is best for you, and it believes that it is good and right to punish you in order to keep you safe.

You have all believed in a punishing God who does not allow you to have the rewards you so desperately crave. You are actually angry at you, this part of you who punishes and controls-by-fear is the God you know. This part is not God in that God rewards and God teaches that all is safe. Fear will make you a "willing" prisoner who will not wish to be free. Once you contact this part of you, you will be in for a big surprise. This part of you will boast and puff up in an effort to seem tough, but this part is only a child yet. It split in childhood and yet, because it split in childhood, it knows that it is God and that God creates. This part of you knows how to create big things and little things in your life because it is so close to childhood that it remembers... it remembers the God force! It has not forgotten the power to create. It has not grown into adulthood; it simply took on the role at a very early age. This part can be your best friend just as easily as it can be your worst enemy.

Get to know you! Know who you are and what is in you. Spend time alone. Explore you! Explore your feelings and your beliefs. Do not be afraid to be alone and do not be afraid to be different. You will be headed in the right direction if you are going within. Within is where you find God. Within is where you find peace. Within is where you find life and within is where you find love!

∞

Once you begin to realize how you are repeating patterns and acting out old thoughts and beliefs, you will want to re-evaluate how you respond. If you are accustomed to doing everything "your way" you can be sure that you are repeating patterns. If you wish to change, you may do so by asking your habitual patterns to come to the surface and leave. You will be most uncomfortable when old patterns surface and you will want to shut them down. Once you have acquired enough light, you will automatically begin to bring old patterns up in order to release them. Do not be afraid to feel the feelings that are trapped in these thought patterns.

Once you feel these feelings you will be allowed to release them. The biggest problem will be in getting you to feel these feelings. You will usually need a trigger to get them moving. This trigger is, of course, going to be something that frightens you. In order to move fear-filled energy you need to stimulate it. When you stimulate fear it moves so it can take on more fear or, in this case, it will move in order to release fear. Either way it must be moved. It does not usually move on its own without being stimulated unless you have an extremely frightened self who constantly re-stimulates fear on its own. This occurs with many schizophrenics and those you would label as paranoid. Once you have become accustomed to moving your own fear it is easily done in the future. You usually need little to no outside stimulation in order to affect your own sense of well-being.

You will find that you are not going to close yourself off from parts of you simply by pushing parts of you away. Fear is in you and it does not leave by pushing it into deeper places. On the contrary; fear will grow and multiply when it is held in. Allow your fears to surface and allow yourself to experience the fear so you can release it. Your first desire will always be to stop fear, to shut it off, to make a go away. I am asking you to feel it in order to heal you. You need to release fear, and fear is an emotional charge. You have many thoughts and beliefs that are fearful, and you will wish to allow them to surface in order to heal. You are the one who is healing, and if you think that you can heal by fragmenting and shoving parts of you away you are quite mistaken. You have been fragmenting and splitting for a very long time. Now it is time to become whole.

When you begin to own parts of you who have been shut down or shut out of your life, you will begin to feel first uncomfortable and then pain and then, as they release their charge, you will feel relief. This relief will be accompanied by your knowingness and your awareness of the much larger picture. Once you learn to see the larger picture, you will be aware of how life works. Most of you are totally "unaware" and this causes a great deal of confusion. When you become "aware," your life will flow. You will live gracefully and you will no longer "blame," for you will have ascended to a much higher level of "understanding." When you understand, you do not get emotionally caught up in who is wrong or right.

Once you attain understanding, you will easily rise above any past confusion. Most of you are in pain caused by holding on to past events. In this pain is the memory of how confused you were, how frightened you were, and how dark the moment may have been for you. All at once you were hurt, and it may have been most unexpected and often it was unwarranted. You will find that you are creating frightening situations in your life now in order to relieve your own fright or fear. What you once took on, you are now letting go of. If you have taken on a great deal of light, you will automatically begin to release your hold on the dark. The dark is hidden in you in order to keep it away from the rest of you. You do not like to touch the fear, pain, confusion, hurt, anger, emotional denial and shame. You want to leave these feelings behind you, and to do so is to fragment and separate.

You are creating toxic waste dumps inside of you. In the same way that toxic waste builds up and seeps into the ground, and enters and pollutes your water, this same toxic buildup is in you and it seeps into all areas of your life. You socialize with others who have their own toxic waste, and you wonder why your relationships end in pain and chaos.

You are all walking around with a time bomb. You carry this electrical charge that builds and requires release. The only way to discharge and release emotional pain is by allowing it to surface. It is causing you pain only because it is buried in you. If it were not buried in you, it could not cause you pain. If you do not want it in you and causing pain for you, then I suggest you allow it to surface, and be patient and kind and understanding as you feel it leave you. Do not act out and do not blame another for hurting your feelings. When your toxic shame is surfacing it will feel like you are being hurt or maybe punished. You are releasing what has been hurting and punishing you.

⚜

As you begin to clear your fear of pain, you will begin to see pain. Pain will come up in you and you will experience it. Once you have cleared your fear of pain, you will be filled with pleasure. Pleasure and pain are the opposite ends of the same line of energy. Most of you have been clearing your pain for some time. You have emotional pain and physical pain and mental pain. You have stress caused by painful situations and you handle your stress by numbing out. You numb out because you do not wish to feel your pain.

Some of you suppress your pain while others feel it strongly. When you meet someone who is suppressing pain, you will understand now why they cannot allow themselves to "feel." If you, on the other hand, meet someone who is "in" their pain, you will know that he or she is releasing a particular pain event that has been held in too long. If you happen to meet someone who sees everything as painful, you may be meeting one who has great pain from past lives and does not know how to release pain.

Pain is a direct result of being stressed. You are all stressed at this time, and our most positive asset is the ability to stay calm. Be calm no matter what occurs. It is in the calm that you will relieve your stress, and stress free living is very close to pain free living. Once you have created an outlet for your pain, by screaming in your car or beating up your bed, your pain will begin to rise up in order to leave. Energy that is being pushed is often ready to surface and only requires a passage in which to move. Once you begin to purposely scream or hit, in order to "vent" your rage and anger, you are showing stressed energy a way out of you.

This is good! Stressed energy does not belong trapped in you and all knotted up. Stressed energy needs to unwind and flow in order to move itself. You can aid yourself in this process by holding healing sessions where you get as angry and hurt as possible, and really begin to move the hurt or pain that is in you. Sometimes a very brief and slight encounter with a situation can cause a tremendous amount of pain to be moved – especially if one is obviously vulnerable at the time. This allows you to be moved (or the energy in you to be moved) at a very powerful rate. This creates a big chain of events that release enough stress that you can usually clear a great deal of energy.

Often a relationship with someone is involved in triggering such events. This is due to the fact that most of you have been in the role of victim in your past, and whether you were hurt emotionally or physically or both; you carry energy from such events. Often you hold on to such energy as a protection. You want a "reminder" so you will never forget and end up in a similar situation.

Now it is time to let go of protection. You no longer require the use of hurtful, painful memories in order to protect yourself from letting it happen again. You are freeing yourself of the past by allowing energy from the past to leave so it does not contaminate the present. We are creating a bright new future for you and, in this bright new future, you do not need nor do you require a pattern of protection from something that was created in your past. You are wiping your slate clean in order to create heaven on earth. Do not be afraid to leave pain and hurt behind. Do not be afraid to see them go and do not be afraid to "feel" them go.

As you release fear of pain, you will be releasing the biggest block in you! Fear of pain affects your health. It affects your level of peace and it very much affects how you love, or better put, how you fear love. You fear pain and do not want to get hurt so you stop loving. You fear pain and do not want to get hurt so you move away from those who can hurt you; and who can hurt you?... anyone; absolutely anyone who takes a mind to, can cause you pain. Why? Simply because you are human and the human condition allows for events which are often inhumane.

You may act godly or you may act manly, but you are still God. You may act inhumanely or monstrously and you are still human. You will find that even your monstrous acts are godly acts because God is everything. So I suggest you let go of all those monstrous things that have occurred in your past and allow them to just "be." Allow everything to just "be." I am God and I allow you to "be" whether you judge it as okay or not. God is not here to be your judge and you are not here to be God's judge. Whether you like it or not *you and God are one!* I do not expect you to understand at this point in your evolution, as you are still very much a caveman. You will evolve and grow out of your wonderment and amazement at how creation works. Once you get evolved, to a level that allows you to think in broader terms, you will see how young and immature you are at this particular time in your evolution.

Once you begin to release enough energy you will feel more aware of creation and you will "feel" your ability to create. You will then begin to let go of your need to judge creation or God, and you will begin to accept creation or God, i.e....... you!

⁂

As you continue to gain trust that you are indeed releasing energy, you will begin to feel comfortable and safe. You will, oh so gradually, begin to clear energy that is trapped in you and you will no longer be upset when energy pops to the surface. You can understand how others react by understanding your own reactions. This is why your number one rule "Do unto others as you would have them do unto you" is so important.

You will find that everything you do is actually run through you first. If you hate someone, then hate runs through you and affects every cell in your body. Thus you now have you hating you. If you seek revenge on another, you start revenge running through your body and affecting every cell in you. Now your body seeks revenge on itself and is put down, or punished, in whatever way your revenge feels is just.

Then, if you seek to be top dog and have everyone else beneath you, you only increase your low self-esteem. This is due to the fact that energy, running through your body, is programming it to fall on its face or not come out on top. You don't consciously think this, but your "desire" is for others to not do as well as you so that you might be the best at something. This causes a message of "failure" to be sent into every cell of your body. This causes you to fail in areas perhaps unrelated to the one you wish to be top dog in. You may get to be top dog at work and fail in other more important ways. This is all due to your way of thinking.

Always, as you think and create, I want you to see everyone the same. If you want to get ahead do not visualize you being the best. Visualize everyone being the best! Competition is creating some pitfalls for you. You no longer focus on yourself and how well you can do, you also focus on your competition and how you want them to fail or simply not be successful. If you do not wish someone to be successful because you do not want to see them do better than you, you are actually programming your body to not be successful. This programs your brain to interrupt success. Do you wonder why you never get ahead in certain areas of your life? It is simply because you have programmed you to not get ahead by wishing someone else would not get ahead.

If you feel angry at your mate for always saying how right he or she is, you are programming yourself to be wrong or to be seen as wrong. If you, just once, want to see he or she fall flat on his or her face so you can feel better about you, you will "fall" because you are programming a fall. You may physically "fall," you may emotionally "fall" into a mild depression, you may literally "fall" from grace or out of grace with your family or a friend. You may "fall" financially in some way or just lose money. You may simply "fall" from a state of happiness into unhappiness.

You are programming you to fall when you want revenge. You are seeking to disempower someone whenever you do not want them to do well in life. This affects them on certain energy levels, and that is why you project such energy at them. It also affects you, and it affects you one hundred times more than it affects them, simply because your energy runs through your body and your body holds on to a great deal of energy because it has been taught to "not let go."

So; if you have been hoping to see someone fail, you will understand why you do not succeed. If you want to succeed in your life, I highly suggest that you begin to see everyone succeeding in their lives. Be generous when you think of others, especially when you think of your enemies. They have a greater charge in your mind than your friends do. Your enemies have affected you in very powerful ways. To reprogram what you think of your enemies will cause huge parts of you to be reprogrammed, simply because your charge concerning your "perceived" enemy is great.

Allow yourself the time you require to heal and begin to see everyone as you. This is the last, vast hurdle for you to cross over. Once you begin to see how you and your neighbor are one, you will begin to change how you think and how you feel about everyone – yes, even killers and rapists. You will begin to know how energy works and you will begin to see how you are all the same body. So, for today, I would like you to go out into your world and treat yourself very well... treat "all" of "you" very well!

❧

*A*s you begin to see how you hurt your own self, you will begin to change. Knowing who you are and knowing what you do allows you to own who you are and what you do. Once you get out of the guilt/blame business you will no longer find it necessary to hurt you or anyone else. The only reason you hurt you is simply because you "blame" you for some judgment you falsely carry. Once you let go of judgment you will let go of blame. Blame is caused by your inability to accept what is.

Once you learn to accept what is, you will begin to feel better about who you are. In accepting, you are releasing blame. In accepting, you are creating flow. In accepting, you are allowing for change. You will want to hold on to blame because you have been taught to blame someone or something. You think it saves you from pain. You do not want to be blamed for anything so why would you want to blame another. When you blame another you are doubly blaming you. Once again, the energy runs through your body, and you "feel" and "wear" and "live with" the impact and the effects of blame. Do you wonder why you feel so hurt if anyone else should blame you for something you judge to be bad? You are already so full of blame from pointing your finger at others that you can no longer bear up under the load that you carry.

So; for now I would like you to take a break from blame. It only causes you problems, and it creates energy blocks that create further pain inside of you. You do not need nor do you require further pain. Pain is trying to rise up in order to change to a much lighter energy. Give pain the opportunity to rise up and leave you. Do not create greater blockages in your body by adding to the already overstressed situation in it. Give you a break by no longer judging anything as bad. Allow all blame to slip away from you. Allow everyone to be God and allow everyone to be about God's work.

Simply do not think of yourself, or anyone else, as anything less than God.

Once you have begun to change how you view creation and God, you will no longer require judgment, and blame will become something that has no power. It is best to allow everyone the opportunity to become God. Godly acts do not make a God. God does not act according to mans laws. God is a creative being with the ability to accept and value all parts of the whole. You are simply focused on one piece of the puzzle and you do not see the entire picture. It is like seeing a dog and thinking it is bad because it barks. Barking is what a dog does. Humans have certain traits that are simply part of human nature. Do not judge you and, especially, do not judge someone else. You create big problems for "you" by doing so. Energy is not prejudiced, and it will not know to not blame or harm the one who sends it. It goes out and circulates, and you are the one it goes out in and circulates in.

Once you learn to deal with and accept your own power to create, you will accept your creations in order to change what you are creating. You may spend your entire life blaming your parents, your teachers, your friends, your lovers, but it is all you creating for you, without you knowing that you are your God in your world.

So; stop blaming you (by blaming them) and stop hurting you (by wanting them to hurt) and you will begin to feel very, very good! This extends to world governments and anyone else you wish to see "fall" or "get theirs." You are the one who will fall and you will get yours! It's not so difficult to understand once you see the big picture and know that you are them. For now, just know that *every* thought that you think is directed at you, simply because it runs through your body and touches your circulatory system and your cells and your nervous system. Thoughts are powerful and thoughts create. Allow your thoughts to create for you and not against you. Allow your thoughts to be for you and not against you, by allowing your thoughts to be for everyone and not against anyone.

There is no way to avoid pain without using your energy to block it. It is going to take some time before you release enough pain to allow your pain to stop, or to become simply a signal once again. As you release your pain you will begin to feel more comfortable. It will become easier to be who you are and you will find yourself enjoying who you are. This will come in small doses at first. As you continue to release pain you will continue to gain enjoyment. The joy has left most of your lives due to the large energy blocks inside of you. If there were no energy blocks inside of you, you would feel joyful and energetic and happy every single moment of every single day.

Do not be upset when energy inside of you begins to move, even when you feel the pain trapped in the energy balls begin to unwind or un-layer. You will find that you may feel quite vulnerable and insecure at these times. You may feel sorrow as the pain begins to untangle everything that is entwined within it. You may feel light-headed and a little dizzy before you begin to clear an energy ball or block. This is due to the toxicity involved in the energy itself, so do not be surprised if you have a little acne, or other small grade infection, at the same time you begin to clear your pain. Sometimes, if the pain is very big and very strongly attached to specific organs or body parts, you may have a large infectious growth. This may be quite painful and may require medical attention.

As you begin to clear any large balls of pain energy, you will find it difficult at first and then, as the energy discharges itself, it will get easier and easier. It is not often that you consciously clear pain, and your body will be *relieved* to know that it is finally being *allowed* to let go of this burden that you carry. It will feel relief as well as comfort. The comfort will not come instantaneously but it will come soon after pain has unwound and begun to leave.

Now; for those of you who believe that you can instantaneously transform into light and have instantaneous bliss – you are right! The only problem is in getting you started. If you figure it out from where you now are, please send signals back to God. You have gone so far into darkness that retrieving you instantaneously would be quite shocking for your nervous system and would create other, greater problems for your physical as well as mental bodies.

You all want instant gratification. What you don't seem to realize is how you layered yourselves in matter. You did not become matter overnight, and you do not seem capable of instant transformation simply due to your depth "in" matter. Suffice to say that you have gotten yourselves covered in mud, and now you expect God to simply "blink" it all away so you can be spirit again. You do not seem to appreciate the fact that you are God, and what you chose to do was to leave God. Your choice! I didn't argue... I gave permission by giving free will!

So; here you sit, all covered in mud and screaming for help. The mud on you is so thick and dried that it is literally caked on and baked in. You are looking for a way out, and you are screaming for help so *here I am!* I ask you to begin to cleanse yourself in order to soften your crust, then I teach you to gradually lift your arms and use your own two hands to take off the layers that trapped you. Why do I not simply "blink" you clean? Matter does not really exist! You created it in your mind and you will un-create it in your mind. I am dealing with an *illusion* that does not exist except for those who believe in it. You dreamed yourselves right into a reality and, in the process; you created this reality for yourselves. Now I am simply saying "back out," reverse your direction and come home to God! Wake up and be conscious once again. I cannot force you to or you will shatter your fragile psyche.

Once you have cleared some of your bigger layers you will be able to chip away the rest of the dried, caked on mud. Once you lose enough crust, you will be able to see through your real eyes and know that this reality was created for "diversity" and enjoyment. It is not a prison and it is not meant to trap you. You will learn to open your real eyes and see again for the very first time in a very long time. You are not clear on what you are and how you behave because you have gotten so deep into matter that you have become a ball of mud. It is very frustrating to be a ball of mud, stuck in a body, stuck in a dimension that exists only in theory. You are not really here... you only think you are....

You will begin to feel as though you have been uncomfortable for a very long time, and then you will begin to feel nervous and uneasy. This is when you know you are about to bring up a deep fear from within you. Sometimes you will be unable to shake the feelings that you are in danger. This is due to the fact that attached to much of your fear is the feeling of threat, or implied threat. If you were once harmed for doing wrong, you will begin to feel as though you can't do anything right. This will cause you to be nervous and on edge. This will in turn cause you to want to move away from your current situation. Often you are projecting old hurts onto current situations. You are being made to feel uneasy by your own fear that is deep within you. As you release this fear, you will ultimately feel better. Often, you will think that you feel better after moving away from the situation, but the situation was only a trigger to get the fear moving in you, so it could rise up out of you.

Now; some of you appear to have greater fear than others. This is due to the fact that some of you are more connected to your own energy and have brought some of your walls down. When you have fewer walls to keep your fear behind, you have greater access to your fear. As you release fear, you actually release a charge that runs through your body and will affect many parts of your body. This charge is usually quite a jolt of electricity and will cause some disturbances along the energy centers of the spine. This is often released through the mucous membranes as well as the lymphatic system. You are constantly clearing and releasing fear, and you are constantly feeling what you are releasing.

Do not worry. You will be better after you have drained the trenches of your subconscious self. You will be happy and you will know peace. It is only a matter of releasing what you carry so that you might be free to carry energy that flows. It is not necessarily a lifetime project. You may reach ascended states in a fairly short period of time. Do not be impatient with yourself and do not be afraid of the fear that is leaving you. Allow it to go and allow you to feel it going. Do not worry that you are losing control. You are not to be in control. Control is how you get to feel safe, and you are learning to give up frightened-controlling in favor of God.

Once you begin to feel the fear rise in you, be as gentle as you can with yourself and with those around you. Fear likes to attack and to blame, as these are its basic energies at this time. Allow your fear to flow from you while you maintain a center of calm. Give yourself lots of time alone to release whatever is coming up, and then stay centered during the day and through your activities.

You might do as my pen has done and actually verbalize with your fear. After all, you have been learning to communicate with all parts of you, and here is a very "big" part of you. So you might want to suggest to your fear that it continue to come up and you will assist it in doing so. You might comment on its progress or even ask how it is doing. This allows your fear to know that it is an accepted part of you. As long as it is accepted it does not feel as though it has to push hard to get through to you. Most fear was conceived during trauma and has spread and grown over time. Trauma leaves little to no time to achieve an accurate perception of the actual incident that created the fear charge to be taken on.

So; if you want to assist your fear in ascension, you may do so by becoming acquainted with it and by acknowledging it. Let it know that you know it exists. Stop hiding your fear from you. Begin to accept it and acknowledge it so that it might come into consciousness and know freedom. Fear has been pushed down in you for so long that it is out of your reach in some cases. Be a friend to you... all of you. Your fear is in you and it makes up a great big part of you.

Get to know fear. Allow fear to leave so that you might create more love. Love does not kill fear. Love is fear and fear is love. It is the same part of you only it has been stretched out of shape. Love shows trust and a willingness to share. Fear is love stretched to the extent that it no longer trusts and it does not know how to share. Mistrust is only fear. Fear is love turned in on itself in order to stop it or block it. If we get hurt by someone, we block the flow of love to that someone. This means that since love moves in us, we block the flow of love to part of us. Fear then replaces love, or, better put, fear becomes a stand-in for love.

Some of you are so full of fear that love has been blocked from every part of you. Once you move fear it will leave a space for love to move in. Everything is energy and everything moves and flows. Try to move and flow with your fear. Try to work with your fear as it escapes you. Try to allow it to use you as it leaves you. It is "in" you and must use your nervous system in order to come up and out. Do not try to stop it. You have spent lifetime after lifetime stopping fear from coming to the surface of you. Let it surface. Let it out. You need not push it down any longer. Do not 'fear' fear. It is energy that wants to leave you and you are ready to rise up also. You will not like to feel fear. You have never liked to feel fear. Fear is a signal just like pain is a signal. You have let pain get distorted and changed beyond recognition. You have also allowed fear to get distorted and changed beyond recognition.

❧

As you learn to move into fear, you will be taking the last step in your healing. Your ability to face your fears is all that is necessary. As you learn to face your fears, you will see how you are actually quite safe in life. Your fear convinces you that you are unsafe. This, of course, means that as your fears surface you will actually begin to feel unsafe. Most of you do not know how to face your fears. You believe that to ride a bull, or jump out of a plane, or go on stage is facing your fears. That is actually overcoming your fear of something. Now you are going to overcome your fear of fear.

As you enter this process, you will see how fear is simply an energy that is running you. As you learn to download your fear you will become accustomed to the flow of fear energy leaving, and your safety will no longer feel so threatened. You will begin to experience performance anxiety, and you will question how well you are doing in life and in your own ability to cope with life. This is a part of releasing pent up fear. These fears have been with you for a very long time and this is why you are so uncomfortable living "in" you.

You will find that, as you release greater amounts of fear, you will begin to trust life, trust yourself, and trust God. You will also begin to know who you are. You will unblock huge areas "in" you that are disconnected from other parts of you simply by this energy buildup and blockage. If you begin to reconnect all parts of you, you then turn on your *creative flow*. This is how you create what you desire. When you are full of fear you automatically shut down your creative flow. You do not trust God and you do not trust being God. To open you up to trust, it is best to open your creative process. Your creative process has been working, but only slightly, and it is tainted by your experiences in both your past and your present. As you allow your fear to surface, it will automatically leave your creative process alone and your creative ability will return to you.

If you are not happy, you will be. If you are not pleased, you will be. If you are not feeling love, you will be! Your creative process is how you operate. When the creative process is blocked, you automatically shut down. You can't feel God. You no longer hear God. You will begin to hear God and to feel God by allowing your fear to leave. Fear has become your God. Fear creates in your life. Fear drives you! You say it doesn't and I say it does. How many of you work for free? You work for money to keep you safe. Money provides food and shelter. If you were given free food and shelter by your government and you were supplied with clothing by simply going into a store and asking, would you still work? No, I do not think you would. If the elderly did not have fear of being rejected and no longer useful, they would not feel the need to work for satisfaction either. It is not that working is bad. I am simply trying to show you how great the fear control is.

It is not necessary for you to quit your job in order to face your fear. That would again be facing your fear of doing something. What I am asking you to do is to allow your fears to surface, and to know that fear is leaving you and not get upset with it for doing so. It has been your captor for so long that you will feel like you are losing something. You are. You will be losing one of the largest parts of you. You will feel sorrow at your loss and you will feel like you want to stop this loss. Do not stop it. Do not try to stuff fear back down inside of you. Allow fear to move up and out, and you will be allowing you to return to your natural state which is love.

You are the love and the light of this world, and the only reason you are not shining brightly is because you have been turned off. I wish you to turn back on so that I might join you. I wish you to allow me to bring you home to love. I wish you to allow me "in" you by allowing fear "out." You can block God simply by not trusting God. You can block love by not trusting love; you can block trust by the fear of trust. Anything you fear is going to be blocked. Right now you are 'fearing' fear. Unblock fear and allow it to release. Fear is blocking everything else that you want.

Once you begin to see how it is not offensive to heal, you will begin to accept the healer in you. You have been taught, or trained, to be a specific way and to not deviate from your current beliefs. If you all of a sudden begin to heal, and you do not allow your beliefs to change first, your healing may simply fade into the past and you become again what you once were. As you heal, your beliefs begin to change in order to allow your cells to change. You are programmed in your cells, and it only makes sense that you will be healed in your cells. As healing takes place you are literally changing your biochemistry, and you are allowing for change elsewhere by changing your biochemistry.

Once you begin to change your biochemistry, you will begin to change patterns within your makeup or your chemistry. You will begin to change you from what you are, into what you are becoming. You are becoming light and you are opening up to change in order to become light. How can you become something you are not if you do not change to become it? You will find that you do not like change. Change often causes discomfort simply by moving you away from what you are accustomed to. I asked you to move out of what you know and into what you do not know. If you were already accustomed to light you would not require healing. You are healing because you are full of pain, and pain comes from programming and your programming is in need of change. So; in order to heal we must change you.

Now; when you begin to change you will not be so certain of who you are. This will be due to the fact that you are changing and are no longer acting or behaving as you once did. We have already discussed how this may affect others, but now we will discuss how this affects you. You will be afraid of this new you, just as your old friends may be afraid of your changes. You will want to be what you are comfortable with and that, of course, is the darkness and pain that you have always carried. We can only take away a little at a time. This is due to the fact that you would freak out, and run screaming away from you if you begin to let go of too much and change too much. So; as a result, these changes go on over a long period of time, and they allow you to adjust to each new loss of pain (your old friend).

So now you are losing bigger and bigger amounts of pain simply because, over a long period of time, you have cleared and released enough to allow bigger and bigger layers to come off of you. This increases your intake of light, and your intake of light increases the ability to release even bigger pain. So; as you begin to release bigger pain you are actually carrying bigger light, which will assist you in releasing bigger pain, as well as in the struggle to "hold on" to the old you or the pain.

As you clear and release bigger pain, your intake of light increases. This intake of light assists you in the release of greater pain, and it assists you in holding yourself in a place of calm so you do not struggle with the pain that is leaving. More light means more peace in times of crisis. Peace is the result of lack of struggle or pressure against something. When you carry big amounts of light you do not get so caught up in the drama of the energy that is leaving you. You begin to see how you can stay calm and all will leave, and you will feel better as a result of allowing pain to leave. Pain and fear are very close, and you are letting go of fear by letting go of pain. Many painful situations have been caused by fear, and fear is going when pain goes. Fear is attached to pain by threads, and fear is a big part of what makes up pain. When you see yourself as "in pain" you are actually "in fear" and fear is causing pain.

So; when you begin to take off bigger layers, you will be balanced by the fact that you take on bigger light. The amount of light you carry is directly related to the amount of pain that you have released. Pain and fear leave and light pours in. This is how it has always worked. What you release is always replaced by something else. If you grow flowers and do not tend to the weeds they may choke the flowers and take over your flower bed. All energy grows and develops. If you do not take out the weeds you cannot plant more flowers. The flowers will flourish and grow if you simply give them water and do not plant weeds next to them. Give them space to grow. They can grow big and strong so that they are immune to weeds. You will find that your light is very fragile, in that it is just now beginning to grow. Do not choke it off. Allow the light in you to grow by continuing to release the pain that you carry.

Allow the light to guide you and allow the trust to develop between you. You have a great bond with pain, and now I would like to see you have a great bond with God. God is the light. God is growing in you. God has come out of the darkness and wishes to be brought forward into your consciousness. Allow God to be "in" you and allow light to be "in" you. You are the light of the world and we are just now turning you on. Let fear go. Let pain go. Do not fear them as they rise up in you in order to leave you. Your light will assist you and your light will grow "in" you, and you will therefore be growing in light!

❧

*O*nce we begin to know how you operate in the "light," it will no longer be necessary for you to operate in the dark. You will, of course, retain your perceptions of what it was like in the dark and it will be similar to the perception you now carry regarding the light. You once walked in the light and you once played in the light, and you had no fear. I know you find this incomprehensible from where you now stand, but it is true. You were and still are pure spirit. You have the ability to turn energy to light or to darkness. You chose darkness out of a desire to try something new. You got bored just "being" and so you decided to explore other options. You really did not get bored, as you never get bored being God. It is more like being "moved." You began to move and it was exciting.

Once you began to move, you felt the need to stop and adapt to your new position. You stopped, and you simply were so in the dark as to who you are that you forgot how to "move" you on. You got stuck where you are and you are just now beginning to move. You are not disabled, and you are not wounded so badly that you cannot return or move on. Some of you want so badly to return that you actually "feel" this possibility. You will soon be returning and you will no longer feel so alone and cast off from God. You will gradually begin to feel how you are gaining "light" and letting go of darkness. You will also find that you are no longer stuck. You will be happy to move into your future and you will not hold on to the present or the past.

As you continue to explore your past, in order to clear and release it, I do suggest you contain yourself and not get too involved. Yes, you have a past and it is thrilling for some of you to see your past lives. Allow this to be an opportunity to heal and release old hurts and pains and fears. Do not play too long in your past lives. You do not need to reacquaint with everyone you knew in a past life. You do not "owe" anything to another. No karmic debt exists unless you make it so. It's just like your present life. If you believe that you owe someone then you are creating that reality for yourself.

What you feel when you meet someone from a past life, or past experience, is recognition. Sometimes recognition is heavily "charged." If the soul you are meeting has killed you in the past, you may feel very uncomfortable. Some of you will feel nothing; however, in others the recognition is strong. If the soul you are meeting once was a parent to you, or otherwise nurtured you, you will feel very drawn and perhaps you will feel that you owe a karmic debt to this soul. That is your choice. There are no rules regarding who you were or who you are now. You create the rules. God simply creates.

Now; for those of you who do not believe in past lives, you will find that you are right also. You see, everyone is right and no one is wrong. Past lives do not really exist and neither do you. It's all an illusion and you created yourself and you are the illusion. So; if you want to use semantics here, you may do so. Just remember that you are trying to figure out how you are what you are, and the instrument you are using to make your calculations is "in" you! You use your reasoning power to make something true or false, and your reasoning power is what creates as it goes. You do not understand the instrument, so how can you read and understand the data.

You are simple; you are complex. You are right; you are wrong. You are God; you are nothing. You are corrupt; you are perfect. How can you possibly figure out anything from where you are? Do not debate! Do not argue. Be!!!

As you learn how to operate your own "creative" energy, you will begin to see how you have always created for yourself. You do not realize how energy works and so you judge your creations and you judge yourself, and you blame your creations as well as blaming yourself. Once you begin to "realize" how thought creates, you will begin to change your thoughts. As long as you are in denial that you are creating your life, your world and your universe, you will continue to create in the dark. As soon as you begin to "realize" how it has always been you doing your creating, you will begin to change what you do not want. All that is in your life will become a "choice" instead of happenstance.

You will begin to see a major shift in how you perceive yourself and this will bring new respect to yourself. A large problem in how you view yourself has to do with lack or loss of self-respect. You do not respect who and what you are, simply because you are so confused about who and what you are. Once you learn to see who you really are, you will begin to appreciate and respect yourself. This ability to respect your own self is something that you have not been taught. You are taught to respect others and to "look up to them." Now I want you to "look up to you." Stop giving your power over to others, and value your own self, based on who you really are. You are the creator of your world. Love your creator.

Now; when you begin to see how you have created some big blocks for yourself, I do not want you to judge yourself for it. Embrace it and know that it was a "good thing." Everything you do is good. You are not here creating bad! There is no bad. You will not fully comprehend this for some time. So, for now, trust me on this one thing. You will all see patterns that you have repeated lifetime after lifetime, and you have repeated these patterns for a reason. They served a purpose, and now you are moving on to the next step or "phase" in your evolution. You will begin to feel as though you are being brought into a total mess when you begin to "clear" your patterns. Do not worry. You are not a total mess; you are simply "blocked" from your source. This block is, and was, necessary. In order to establish a hold in the dark you must pretend to be dark.

So; now you sit in the dark and you brave explorers are afraid and you want out. This was expected and we do have a backup plan. Here is our backup plan: You will now love you regardless of anything you have done this life. You will also respect you, no matter what you begin to see regarding your ignorance. After all, if you are God, you are pure light intelligence and that means you make no mistakes; everything is in divine order; you are in divine order.

So; as you dig up your dysfunctional patterns, you will begin to see a few things you do not like about yourself. I will tell you now that, as surely as I sit here writing this book, I am the first to "allow" you to expand and be all that you are. So; if you feel that you made a big mistake in your life – you did not! If you feel you should have done other than what you did – you should not. It is not important how awful you may have been. Judgment does not allow for mistakes, and when you are God – there are no mistakes.

So; as you begin to uncover your patterns, I want you to allow yourself respect due God! You are God. You have very intelligent reasons for creating, and you have intelligence beyond your capacity to understand. You are a very microscopic pinpoint of light. You do not have access to the "whole" and so you are limited. You are separated from your source by your ability to separate. Do not judge separation. I want you to come home and I want you to become whole. I also want you to embrace separation and fragmentation. You are all! You are not one or the other. You are everything, and to embrace all of you is to embrace "all." Nothing gets left out.

❧

You will begin to see how you are God by looking at how you create. Once you see how you create undesirable situations for yourself you will want to change. This is how you now create: you see something you want, you then go after it and if you do not get it you are upset and often angry. You are at your infancy phase of creating. Once you learn how often your belief in punishment stops you from getting what you want, you will see how you can change in order to receive. As you use punishment for bad and reward for good it is only natural that you let go of both.

Once you begin to simply be, you will see big changes in how you create. Right now you are creating so much tension and pain, by pushing you to do better, that you are receiving punishment instead of reward. You do not receive what you want by pushing you to do better. You are simply running energy through your body that says, "I am not good enough, I do not do well enough." This translates within the body to two messages "not good" and "not well." How many of you "feel" these two messages in yourself? Once you learn to stop sending such messages you will actually begin to heal. It takes a long time to heal if you have put in a lifetime of negative messages, so please be patient with the patient.

As you begin to see how you are creating, you will be allowed to accept your responsibility for creation. Once you learn how you create, you can learn how to re-create any situation with a more pleasurable outcome. This takes a little practice and will be most appreciated by you. It is the ability to reward yourself for being who you are. It is not necessary to reward only good deeds, as "good deeds" creates a space or void to be filled called "bad deeds." Do not believe in reward and punishment. Believe in reward for simply being and reward for simply breathing. If you are here, give yourself a reward. Do not be so cynical as to believe that you do not deserve if you do certain things.

You cut off your supply of good to you by cutting off your supply of good to another. Do not judge in this way. Allow everyone to simply be who they are. Do not reward some with your love and select others to punish with your disgust and anger. You are only selecting parts of you (inside your own cells) to receive your disgust and anger. You are dying of disease because you are killing your cells with disgust and anger. You loathe others and this intense feeling affects you not them. You hurt you by your dislike of them. Your cells receive the message, "I hate you; I cannot stand you. Go away, get out of my life." And so your cells get infected and they die. You are killing you with your thoughts. You do not know how to love.

You will find that, as you begin to love, you will begin to see a great change in your own life. Whatever you give is given only to you. Whatever you receive is a gift. If you die it is often not punishment. Often the death of the body is a release from punishment. Often the body simply shuts down in order to stop pain. It is so full of abuse that it is dying and, in some cases, it is not at all what it once was. In some cases your bodies are made of chemicals and compounds that do not belong in them. They are breaking down their own organic matter in order to please you. You put chemicals in them and you willingly poison them, and you still expect them to perform. This is not a judgment against you. This is straight informative information. You will not allow me to talk straight with you, as you do not care to hear how you are causing your own demise. You prefer to blame God when a loved one dies. You even blame God when you get seriously ill.

I will tell you now; you are killing you and it does not really matter except to you. You are part of nature and matter. You do not like to die. You are going to die unless you take responsibility for your actions against your body. Begin to love your body. Begin to respect your body. If you meet someone who tells you

The Grace is Ours

that you need not respect life, I suggest you tell that person they are disrespecting God. I am in you. I am you.

※※

Once you begin to see the difference between how you are versus who you are, you will become acquainted with the real you. You are who you are by birth, and you are how you are by traits given to you. You will begin to let go of your traits in order to be who you are. Your traits are not really who you are. Your traits often impair who you really are. As you become more acquainted with who you really are, you will find it easier to release your traits. This is also true for your friends. You do not find certain traits acceptable and yet you know that the actual person is not his or her traits. Once you learn how to distinguish between a person's traits and her ability to be real, you will not find certain behaviors so upsetting. You are all capable of deceit, and the one you most often deceive is you.

When you begin to open up to consciousness you will feel less than adequate. You will begin to feel less than yourself, and this is partly due to the fact that you are letting go of parts of you that no longer support where you are going. These may be as simple as small traits or as large as big character flaws. Once you learn to wake up, you no longer feel the need to walk in armor and this allows you to lighten up and be freer. You will find that, as you walk down your chosen path, you will leave parts of you and you will retrieve parts of you. You are the one who decides what to retrieve and what to leave. You are the one who is creating you and re-creating you. You are the one who asks for help, or does it on your own. You are the one who makes you one way or the other way. You decide who you will appear to be and you decide what traits you will carry.

Now; if you do not agree with what I have just said, I suggest that you remember how you choose your parents, your neighborhood, your family, your hair color, your body type and your belief system, be it religious or nonreligious. You choose your traits carefully before you enter form. You see your entire life unfold before you agree to play the role. You are not forced to be you, quite the contrary. You ask to be whomever you choose. You do not get tricked into being you. You volunteer and you sign up and you request to be you.

So; if you want to be you, and if you see your life played out in advance, and if you are chosen by you, how could you be in the wrong place at any given time? If you are mugged, you saw it before hand. If you are raped, you saw it before hand. If you are killed, you saw it coming. If you are abused, you knew it was there in the life pattern that you personally handpicked for you. There are no accidents. You knew then, and parts of you know now. I am not trying to blame you for your choice. I am only saying that you made a good choice for you. You do not stumble by accident into a body, or a life, or a situation. You set it up. You saw it coming.

You are experimenting in matter. You are not experimenting on you. You are experimenting from within you on this thing you call matter. You are not being punished; you are simply feeling like you have no control. I am simply giving your power back to you by saying, "You are the creator of the whole show." You are the one in charge. You are the head honcho and you have forgotten who you are. You think that you have become what you appear to be. You have not. You are the power behind life. You are the source. You have lost your connection with you. You are inside of you and you are very much in control.

This you is having difficulty due to distance. Your distance is due to invisible walls placed between you and you. You are in you. You are part of you. You are divine. You are not evil. You are not garbage. You are the "light" that permeates space. You are the electricity that turns on matter. You are the space and the matter but you feel like nothing. This is due to the fact that you have not "felt" who you are in a very long time. You have been asleep. Now you are waking up and you may feel groggy and out of sync at first. You are not falling apart, you are simply becoming aware. First you had to become aware that you had a body. This takes some time. Now you must become aware that your body is not real and you are the space that holds it in place. You are not so much the space that holds it together as you are the "light" that holds it together.

So; do not judge you as you have handpicked everything about you, and do not fear waking up as it too was handpicked by you. You will learn how to ascend and you will learn how to be God. It's not so difficult. You unlearned it and now we will start again and relearn it. You are in a very special place. Inside of you is all the information you will ever need. Inside of you is the coded and encoded wisdom of eternity. Inside of you is the "light" of the world. Inside of you is a gold mine of informative wisdom. Inside of you are all the secrets you keep from yourself. Inside of you, you will find "peace," you will find "love," you will find "joy," you will find "tolerance," you will find "acceptance," you will find "God." If I were you, I would thank God that I am you and I would take very extra special care of everything that is inside.

⚜

Once you begin to realize how you are God, you will begin to take good care of you. You will stop criticizing you (and everyone else) and you will stop bossing you around (as well as everyone else). You will begin to change how you see yourself and you will change how you see the world in general. Once you see how you are God, you will become "content" to be God. You will give up your struggle and you will begin to feel "hope." Hope will bring you into "grace," and in grace you will find your "pleasure." Grace is how you will know life. You will move in grace and you will be protected by your ability to stay in grace. You will feel blessed and you will no longer feel like a victim in life.

As you learn to be God, you will wish to thank God for the ability you have. This gratitude will add to you as you feel it running through you. This gratitude will keep you in a state of acceptance, which will assist you in receiving even greater gifts. As you take on this feeling of gratitude or appreciation, you will begin to feel appreciated. It will be you receiving you! This is how you get to be God. If you deny you, you will never receive you. In denying who you are, you only push at you and this separates you further. If you accept you as

God, you allow parts of you to merge and become one. You reconnect with who you are; your source; your creator. You are all part of the same creator and you all carry parts of you that are not to your liking. In creating you, you accepted these parts.

As you grew less tolerant you began to expel or dismiss more and more parts. These fragmented parts contain you. These fragmented parts contain your life force. These fragmented parts are left alone to survive and exist in a state of exile. If you do not come out of denial you will continue to expand on a material level while getting even smaller on a spiritual one. You will continue to send away parts of you and these parts contain God.

You are God. You forgot that you are, and now you are splitting off and multiplying in such tiny fragments that you are losing your ability to hold light. Your ability to hold light is what keeps you in the light. It allows you to "feel" light and to love. You have been so fragmented that you do not feel the heat of love. Light is like a fire that warms you. Your fire is dying simply because you have spread yourself out for miles by separating and splitting. Once you begin to arrive back home or back in you, you will begin to feel the warmth again. You will calm down and not feel so cold.

As you begin to regain your light, you will begin to feel grace. Grace is the ability to remain a light. Grace is the easy flow of light. Grace is being blessed and knowing it; feeling it. When you are blessed and you do not know it or feel it, you are not connected to your blessings and they simply go unnoticed and underappreciated. Once you are connected, you begin to see the miracles of life.

In the beginning of this series I explained to you that Liane, my pen, was in a state of grace. She was put in such a state in order to show her how life could be for her, if she chose to continue to walk in faith and to continue to draw parts of herself back to her. She has continued and now she is oh so gradually beginning the first phase of creating grace. She was held in grace in order to begin this project, and now she is returning to that same state simply by her ability to "desire" it. It has happened for many of you. You see miracles and feel God's presence very strongly and then you begin to clear and release your debris.

The main "desire," which is your strongest creative force at this time, is to return to "light" or that feeling of "grace;" that feeling of God's presence in your daily life. You felt it once and it felt so good to you that you will do anything, no matter how long it takes, to get back to that feeling. This is how you return on your own and create a big space in you to be filled with light. You are working for God and you do not know that you are. You are adding to you by wanting your life to be free of pain and struggle. You are adding to you by allowing pain and struggle to rise up in you and leave you. You are creating space for "light" right inside of you. You may spend many years re-collecting parts of you and they are never wasted years. You are building a big fire inside of you that will burn brightly and warm you for eternity.

Once you know how God works, you will understand how you work. It is not as it seems. You are doing God's work and you think you are all messed up. You are not all messed up. You are, however, cleaning out the mess to create harmony, which will allow for peace, and peace will allow for pleasure and pleasure will allow grace on a steady basis.

❧

*A*s you take on greater amounts of light, you will begin to feel like you can handle anything. You will normally be energized in a very subtle way. You will not feel frenzied but you will feel energy moving in you. It's sort of like being drawn through something rather than pushing through or fighting against it. You just get oh so gently drawn right through a difficult situation or experience. You will find that, as you are drawn in this manner you will begin to trust life. It will feel more like you are being supported by life and less like you are fighting or struggling for survival.

As you continue to grow in light you will be most comfortable with life. Life is only your frame of sorts. Life allows you to express who you are. Life is the canvas and you are the painter, and you choose your colors and your scene. When you begin to choose "light," you will begin to paint with grace and with ease. You will be in the "flow" and this puts the "flow" in you. You will begin to take on new meaning to yourself, and you will become most conscious of this energy that is "flowing" through you. You will begin to see small changes at first and then you will see big changes.

Once you get the big changes, you will begin to truly feel "joy." You will feel splendid and you will love yourself and everyone around you. This is how you will know that you have "arrived." You will be taken on a journey into and through your own "self" and then, once you have accepted all parts of your "self," you will be allowed to love your "self." This will truly change you. This is transformation!

Is it pleasant going into the judged-as-unpleasant parts of the "self?" No, it is not. Does it take some effort on your part? Yes, some but not a great stretch for you. Will you be happy as you sort through your unhappy feelings and emotions and fears? No, I can't see that happening. Will you be glad you came "into" your "self" or will you be upset and angry? At first you will be glad, then your joy will turn to confusion and possibly anger as you learn to look at how you have created your "self." But in the end, when you have released enough darkness and you begin to feel the light flow within you, you will love what you have accomplished. Yes, it is difficult to take charge of one's own salvation by giving up (or over) control to one's soul, however, it is very, very rewarding.

Once you have learned how to live in the light it will not have such an energy drain on you. You will embrace the light in the same way that you have always embraced the darkness. You will begin to live life through the eyes of love and compassion, rather than through the eyes of fear and control. You will be headed in the opposite direction you were headed. You will be rising up instead of spiraling down. For each of you this will mean something different because each of you created your own path into darkness. This allows each of you to un-create and re-create in your own way. No two of you are expected to feel, think, or understand all of the same techniques, so please allow everyone to have their own personal technique and their own personal experiences. God is inside of everyone, not just you. God is guiding everyone, not just you. God is in charge and you can let go of the reins and allow God to guide "all" of God's children.

I thank you for your advice on how I should or should not do this, but I think I shall allow "free will." Free will does have benefits that you seem to enjoy and I do not wish to become a controlling lord over his slaves. This is God speaking with and through his children. These books are a gift to you through the free will choice of my pen to do this work. The effects are far reaching and many of you will begin to communicate with God. This will be a very good time for all. I will now end this, our twentieth book. I have a great deal more to say, however, Liane has spent the last ten years putting my words on paper and it is time for her to have a short vacation. I will allow her the rest she requires and then I will return.

God – are you finished?

Yes this will be the last book for now, Liane. I am not leaving you; I am only taking a break from writing. This will be good. We will work together again on other books. I will tell you when. Thank you for your help.

From the Pen

I didn't know God would have so much to say! I started to write for God thinking he was going to write one book. Then I thought three books. Then, after he started Book 4, I was told by a friend that it would be three sets of three books, a total of nine. Well, you can imagine my surprise as he just kept urging me to write until I had written twenty books containing over six thousand handwritten pages. I was amazed! I'm still amazed!

So; how do I do this? I still do not know. I thought at first that I was like an extension cord. I could plug into an outlet (the Source) and the electricity (information) would run through me and onto the page. Since then I've changed my mind and decided that the information is somehow contained inside of me and I assume it's in everyone and everything.

God told me that he has a great deal more informative, intelligent information and could write for my entire life and not run out of information. So I said, "Let's do it." I sure hope he wants to use me some more....

Liane

"God, use me…"

Sometimes I ask God to use me or work through me. A few weeks ago I was in one of those places where you have to take a number and wait for your number to be called before you can be helped. I sat next to a lady with a very cute baby that began to cry. The mother took the child outside and a man sat down next to me. He smelled of cigarette smoke and could have used a bath, so I opened the book I had brought to help me pass the time and began to read.

The man began to ask me questions, and I answered as briefly as I could and went back to my book in an effort to avoid him. He was persistent and even nudged me on the shoulder good naturedly. As I was trying to read my book, and ignore his presence, my God voice went off and said, "You're always asking what you can do." I wasn't sure what God meant by that, and shrugged it off as the man began asking me what I was reading and why I had post-its on many of the book pages. I showed him the book title, and answered nicely that those post-its marked the pages I wanted to go back to and read later. I then politely ignored him and returned to my book. Again God said, "You're always asking what you can do." I then got it! I thought, "Oh there's going to be a gift in this." So I closed my book and gave this person my full attention.

Well, he talked about wanting to quit smoking and how he had gone from several packs to just one pack a day. He also talked about wanting to quit drinking and how he doesn't normally drink until after 6:00 PM, but this morning he just had to have a rum and coke (his favorite drink) to calm his nerves. He talked about wanting to move to Japan and mentioned how he felt like that was his home and he should have been born there instead of the U.S. Mostly, he talked and I just listened. It did make the forty-five minute wait seem like just fifteen minutes.

So, on the drive home I'm talking to God in my car and laughingly I say, "So what was that about?" And God says, "Well, you're always asking me to use you and sometimes the only way I can give love to a human is through another human."

God's Pen

I first heard the voice of God in 1988. I was sitting in my back yard reading a book when this big booming voice interrupted with, "I am God and I will not come to you by any other name." I felt like the voice was everywhere – inside of me as well as in the sky around me. I was so frightened that I ran in my bedroom to hide.

This was not the first time that I heard voices. I had been communicating with my own spirit guide or soul for about a year. I guess my depth of fear regarding God, and all that he represented to me at the time, was just too much.

I spent two days trying to avoid the voice of God, which was patiently waiting for me to respond. By the second day I was exhausted from lack of sleep and decided to give in and talk with him. This turned out to be the greatest gift and best decision of my life.

The first book, *God Spoke through Me to Tell You to Speak to Him*, shows my evolution from communicating with my soul to communicating with the Big Guy. It took a couple years for me to be comfortable communicating with God. My fear of a punishing God was big! That has most definitely changed and I now think of God as my partner and best friend.

In the beginning the voice of God would wake me in the middle of the night and tell me it was time to write. He said I had promised to do this work (I assumed he was talking about the soul/spirit me). I would drag myself up to a sitting position and watch in amazement as my hand flew across the page, while I tried to keep up by reading what was being written.

It was always so much fun to wake up the next morning and grab my notebook to see what God had written during the night. After some time the voice stopped waking me and I became comfortable picking up my pen and writing for God first thing in the morning. I think in the beginning I had to be awakened while still semi-conscious from sleep so I wouldn't object too much to the information that was being channeled through me.

As I grew less and less afraid (and more trusting) of God, he was able to communicate greater information. Some of the information is quit controversial, but I felt it important to just let it be and not censor it. I present the writings here to you as they were given to me. I have edited a little (mostly the more personal information regarding myself) and I have used a pen name for privacy reasons. I asked God for a good pen name and he guided me to Liane which (I was told) in Hebrew means "God has answered."

At one point I became a little concerned about my sanity in all this, so I went to a hypnotherapist to find out what I was doing. Under hypnosis I saw this incredibly huge beam of light with a voice coming from within it. It was a giant "loving light" and felt so comforting and kind. It felt like that's where I came from. After that I stopped worrying about my sanity. If this is crazy, I think it's a very good kind of crazy to be....

In loving light, Liane

Loving Light Books

Available at:
Loving Light Books: www.lovinglightbooks.com
Amazon: www.amazon.com
Barnes & Noble: www.barnesandnoble.com

Also Available on Request at Local Bookstores